MARKETING

A STRATEGIC PERSPECTIVE

MARKETING

A STRATEGIC PERSPECTIVE

James M. Hulbert
PROFESSOR OF BUSINESS
COLUMBIA UNIVERSITY

Foreword by William K. Brandt
MANAGING PARTNER

IMPACT PLANNING GROUP

Published by Impact Publishing Company
A Division of Impact Planning Group
P.O. Box 244
Katonah, NY 10536

Library of Congress Catalog Card Number: 85-80154
ISBN 0-9614952-0-0

Printed in United States of America
First Printing

Dedicated to the
Memory of my
Beloved Mother
Ruth Constance Ivy Hulbert

CONTENTS

FOREWORD

Since World War II the development of marketing as we know it can be separated into two distinct periods: thirty years of relative expansion, mild inflation and inexpensive capital, followed by a decade of lackluster growth, high inflation and expensive funds.

A snapshot of marketing during the first period revealed the following general conditions:

- The marketing orientation though espoused since the mid-fifties did not represent the *sine qua non* for survival. Academics and executives worked the term into textbooks and annual reports but rarely into managerial decision-making.

- Planning started to move from a quarterly to an annual and longer-term perspective, but in many cases it had little or no effect on day-to-day activities. Long-range plans focused on facility expansion and were driven largely by financial considerations. Annual plans centered on budgets with action programs designed to justify the forecasts and expenditures.

- Many companies began to recognize the need to study customer values, but few made serious efforts to assess their competitors' future strategies. The perspective of the competitor as an enemy was rare.

- Managers hewed to a narrow view of the marketing mix, with industrial companies emphasizing pricing and selling decisions and consumer-product firms focusing upon advertising and sales promotion.

This brief description of marketing from the mid-forties until the mid-seventies does not imply that marketers were unsophisticated, undedicated or deliberate suboptimizers for their employers. Indeed, in many cases this approach was sufficient to prosper in the relatively benign, high-growth markets that existed during this period.

The turmoil which followed the oil shocks in 1973 demonstrated, however, that the old ways would no longer suffice. As one manager cautioned me, "Growth masks many sins; it covers mistakes." Practices and orientations that were adequate in the past no longer applied in the new environment.

The marketing orientation, often described as taking an outward look at customers and competitors, must, in this contemporary environment, become an attitude set or value system that pervades all functions of the business. Planning which is truly strategic must be market-based, matching market opportunities with internal capabilities. The numbers-crunching, blank-filling routine which persists in some companies, must give way to the development of effective strategies which produce prosperity, not mere survival. In well-managed firms annual business and marketing plans are linked with longer term strategies and translate into supporting action programs for the sales force, service, and advertising, and other functions to ensure implementation of strategies.

Competitor analysis has begun to equal customer research as a critical prerequisite for strategy design. The techniques and approaches for customer and competitor assessment have exploded in number, sophistication and frequency of use.

Furthermore, most marketers now appreciate the breadth and power of marketing tools available to create effective strategies. Refinements of offers to specific and often small market targets incorporate far more than price and sales force considerations.

This book focuses squarely on marketing in the brave new world I have outlined. Professor James M. Hulbert started his teaching career in the late sixties, and has lived through the changes described earlier as teacher, consultant, researcher, and practitioner. The book reflects an intimate knowledge of the "real world," while resting on solid theoretical underpinnings.

For managers who have wrestled with the problems of understanding and implementing the marketing orientation, this book should come as welcome relief. It reflects the enormous experience of Professor Hulbert and his colleagues at Columbia University and Impact Planning Group. Through teaching and consulting, these professionals have worked directly with managers to create and sustain a marketing orientation and to develop marketing strategies and programs that pass the reality test in the market.

For students at the graduate and undergraduate levels, the book affords a rather different set of benefits. Unlike many marketing textbooks, this one does not incorporate all there is to know about marketing; instead, it emphasizes what is important to know about marketing. Unlike many authors, Professor Hulbert is not afraid to take a position on what he believes should be done. His prescriptive approach, after the diagnostic overview, is both instructive and refreshing. For the practitioner and student alike, Professor Hulbert presents a clear vision of what marketing should be in a market driven organization.

Professor Hulbert has organized the book to maintain the interest of readers at all levels of experience. He quickly outlines the basic precepts of marketing management and proceeds to develop a consistent set of approaches to address the critical decision areas faced by marketing managers. The lessons and experiences incorporated in this book afford instructive insights for actual and would-be managers of all functional backgrounds.

William K. Brandt
New York City
March 1985

PREFACE

Marketing is at once the most subtle and complex and yet one of the most simple functions of the business enterprise. Subtle and complex because understanding the nuances of customer behavior is a challenge both intriguing and never-ending. Simple because it rests upon fundamental precepts which possess a commanding logic of their own. Perhaps for these reasons, it is all too easy to pay lip service to its importance, yet fail to practice successfully what is so evidently crucial to business success.

Whilst I would not claim that this book will immediately solve the problem, it does focus upon the practical requirements of implementing the marketing concept. While theory is not neglected, it is reflected in the mirror of experience, taking a form which is more closely related to the decisions which managers must take if they wish to build an effective marketing organization. If this work can make a small contribution to the better practice of marketing, my primary objective will have been fulfilled.

The completion of any book involves the contributions of many, besides the author. My dedication of this book to my mother, who died before it was published, was more than a symbolic act, however. There is no doubt in my mind that she and my late father made the most important contribution to its completion. Without the selfless support which my parents gave me in pursuing my education and my chosen profession, I have no doubt that I would not have written this book, nor any other. They say that gratitude is usually expressed too late and too sparingly, and such is unfortunately the case.

I also wish to acknowledge the tremendous intellectual debt I owe to my colleagues, at Columbia and elsewhere. The demanding and brilliant thought of the late Professor Abraham Shuchman was a crucial and formative influence on my thinking about marketing management. The inspiration and support provided by Professor John Howard was vital in motivating me to finish the manuscript. The sustained quality of my professional relationships with my other academic colleagues, notably Professors John Farley, Donald Lehmann, Noel Capon, Russell Winer, Donald E. Sexton and Morris Holbrook, have also been influential in my thinking.

Yet, it would be unfair to include only my academic associates among those whom I should thank. First, I owe much to my partners at Impact Planning Group, Dr. William Brandt and Mr. Robert Christian. A wealth of experience in applying marketing concepts to the solution of real world problems is reflected in the insights and contributions provided by Bill. Bob's penchant for logical and rigorous thinking has forced me into more systematic and structured organization of my thoughts, even though they doubtless still fall short of his very high standards. Finally, it would be remiss of me not to acknowledge the intellectual debt I owe to the countless thoughtful executives and students with whom I have discussed and debated marketing concepts over the years. I hope that in reading the book, the reader will find that at least a little of the wisdom thus gleaned has rubbed off.

Finally, I must express my heartfelt thanks to those whose labor was as important to the publication of this book as my own. For typing, editorial and administrative help, thanks are due to Ms. Elizabeth Blair, Mrs. Barbara Thompson and Ms. Harriet Leonard. For both emotional support and substantive help, my wife Professor Madge M. Lyman, deserves enormous credit. Finally, for their efforts in turning my manuscript into a finished product, I wish to thank Ira Ungar and Joe Friedman. Naturally, responsibility for errors and omissions remain mine.

James Hulbert
Litchfield, CT
March 1985

MARKETING

A STRATEGIC PERSPECTIVE

If we want to know what a business is we have to start with its purpose. And its purpose must lie outside of the business itself. In fact, it must lie in society since a business enterprise is an organ of society. There is only one valid definition of business purpose: to create a customer. [*]

[*] Peter F. Drucker, *The Practice of Management*, New York: Harper and Row, Publishers Inc., 1954, p. 37.

1

THE CONCEPT
OF MARKETING

Marketing is probably the most misunderstood, most difficult to master and, therefore, most poorly practiced activity of the business firm. Our objective in writing this book is to correct the misconceptions, assist in the development of a better understanding of marketing, and improve the quality of practice. These are the ambitious but, we believe, feasible goals to which we address ourselves in the pages which follow.

THE MEANINGS OF MARKETING

There is much confusion over what the word marketing means. This is an inevitable result of the many ways in which the word has been used by both academics and businessmen.

To the housewife, marketing means going to the shop to purchase her household requirements. To the diehard consumer activist, the name may connote a variety of evils, each as pernicious as the other. To management, however, there are three important meanings of the term marketing.

First, marketing is used to refer to the activities which are carried on within the responsible *function, group* or *department* within the firm. Such specific yet diverse activities as advertising, promotion, distribution management, selling, customer service, collection, marketing research, pricing and new product development, for example, may conceivably be grouped together within a firm's organizational structure under the panoply of marketing. These kinds of activities are vital to the firm, are the key

1

concerns of most marketing managers, and will constitute an important part of this book.

Second, we often treat the word "marketing" synonymously with the word "economic" when we talk of the *marketing system*. We might think of this as a macro rather than a micro view of marketing, one which is focussed on the societal role of marketing. Likewise, this is an important aspect of marketing, arguably the most important from the perspective of the nation's political economy, for the marketing system is that which creates and delivers a society's standard of living, both quantitatively and qualitatively.

The third meaning of marketing, however, is the one with which we shall be most concerned in the first part of this book and the one which is by far the most important in understanding marketing strategy. This is the meaning of marketing as a concept and philosophy of management, the meaning to which most people refer when they talk of the *marketing concept* or the *new marketing concept*. Because it is a very fundamental concept, it affects almost every decision which is made in the firm. In consequence, it represents a philosophy which must be known and understood by managers outside of the marketing function—and it is for such reasons that we elevate this meaning of marketing to a position of primary importance in this book.

THE MARKETING CONCEPT

The marketing concept is a concept of what a firm should be and how that firm should be managed. Note that it is a concept of the firm, *not* of a function or department. Its implications are, therefore, far-reaching indeed. This point is not well understood in many companies, whose managers then make the unfortunate mistake of assuming that marketing (in the broad sense) is a job that can be delegated to the marketing department. It is not. To operate with the marketing concept requires a thorough understanding and commitment throughout the business enterprise—not just in the marketing department.

What then, is the nature of this marketing concept, that it can serve as a philosophy of management? Quite simply, the idea at the core of the marketing concept of the firm is that a business exists for the purpose of creating and continuing to create customers. This basic concept provides an organizing framework upon which a whole system of management precepts can and will be built as we progress through this book. We shall call a company operating under this concept a marketing-oriented firm, and shall explore the implications of this orientation in considerable depth.

The Evolution of the Marketing Concept

At first sight, the marketing concept probably seems radically new to many readers. In fact, there are no necessary conflicts between this and more traditional views of the firm. Indeed, although the marketing orientation is only one of the many that might be adopted by the firm, as we shall now see, this concept evolved not out of magnanimity to customers, but from sheer economic necessity.

Robert J. Keith, past President of Pillsbury Corporation, a major U.S. food corporation, described the evolution within his company as follows. First, in the early days of the company manufacturing reigned supreme.

The idea for the formation of our company came from the *availability* of high-quality wheat and the *proximity* of water power.[1]

TABLE 1-1 Evolving Philosophy of Pillsbury Corporation[6]

Era	Philosophy	Orientation
1869-1930	We are professional flour millers. Blessed with a supply of the finest North American wheat, plenty of water power, and excellent milling machinery, we produce flour of the highest quality. Our basic function is to mill high-quality flour, and of course (and almost incidentally) we must hire salesmen to sell it. Just as we hire accountants to keep our books.	Production
1930-1950	We are a flour milling company, manufacturing a number of products for the consumer market. We must have a first-rate sales organization which can dispose of all the products we can make at a favorable price. We must back up this salesforce with consumer advertising and market intelligence. We want our salesmen and our dealers to have all the tools they need for moving the output of our plants to the consumer.	Sales
1950	The company's purpose (is) no longer to mill flour, nor to manufacture a whole variety of products, but to satisfy the needs and desires, both actual and potential, of our customers.	Marketing

In Keith's view, it was resource availability that prompted Charles A. Pillsbury to go into business in 1869, and this orientation sustained the company for many years. Table 1 gives Keith's description of the company philosophy during this era, and describes the evolution. As the environment changed in the early 1900's, so too did Pillsbury and by the 1930's the company had entered the era of sales.

For the first time, we began to be highly conscious of the consumer, her wants, and her prejudices as a key factor in the business equation.[2]

The transition experienced by Pillbury was shared by many other companies during the same time period, as the world's economies experienced the Great Depression. Suddenly, resources were not the key scarcity, customers were.

In the 1950's Pillsbury again saw the need for change — this time toward a marketing orientation. The next step came "with the realization that research and development could produce literally hundreds of new and different products."[3] With such a wide range of possibilities, Pillsbury

... faced for the first time the necessity for selecting the best new products. We needed a set of criteria for selecting the kind of products we would manufacture. We needed an organization to establish and maintain these criteria, and for attaining maximum sales of the products we did select.[4]

With the perhaps excessive enthusiasm that often accompanied the first embracing of the marketing concept, Pillsbury decided to establish a marketing department, "a new management function which would direct and control all the other corporate functions from procurement to production to sales."[5]

While this last step was in retrospect only the beginning of what is often a difficult process involved in implementing the marketing concept, Pillsbury was, of course, not alone in shifting its orientation in the way described above. In the period immediately following World War II, there was enormous pent-up demand among consumers. Although the necessary purchasing power was slower to recover in some countries than it was in others, the flush of deprived demand rendered business prospects quite favorable for many U.S. and some European firms. Underlying these short-term changes, however, was a much more significant concern. For as living standards improved, first in the U.S., then in Europe, it became increasingly clear that a larger proportion of consumers' budgets would become discretionary. Basic needs for food, shelter, clothing and health care would be requiring an ever-smaller proportion of consumer budgets, at least for the developed economies. Thus, whereas at lower levels of economic development firms could rest assured that increases in purchasing power would be translated into purchase, *by necessity*, it now was becoming a matter of volition instead.

The challenge to business, then, would increasingly become how to tempt consumers into choosing to spend money which they did not have to spend. And, in the increasingly competitive environment which characterizes economies of affluence rather than scarcity, the challenge to the individual firm became how to induce those customers to purchase from it rather than the competition. As these changes took place in the business environment, then, many companies began to recognize that their customers would be playing a much more pivotal role in management's decision-making in the future than they had in the past. While some embraced this idea with more enthusiasm than others, a slow dawning of the importance of customers to the firm had begun.

THE MARKETING CONCEPT AND THE PROFIT MOTIVE

It is often alleged that the flaw of the marketing concept is its lack of emphasis upon the firm's own objectives and, in particular, upon profit. It is certainly true that many early proponents of the marketing concept failed to grasp the significance of profit-making, leading their companies into profitless volume growth and product proliferation. In our view, however, those who find this flaw with the concept, or believe that profit is unimportant to marketing-oriented firms, misunderstood the concept itself.

To begin at the beginning, any capitalist textbook in micro-economics will assume (and, in more polemical tomes, advocate) that profit maximization is the appropriate objective of the business activity. We do not argue here that profit is unimportant — but it is important to place the profit objective into the proper perspective. First, we should be aware of the fact that while short-run profit maximization rules are relatively easy to construe, long-run profit maximization remains in practice a much more nebulous and uncertain prospect. Simon's[7] concept of bounded rationality leads to the notion of attaining satisfactory profit levels as a much more valid working assumption. Simon's conception is not too far removed from the way in which we shall treat profit objectives here, *viz.* profits are necessary precisely in order to survive. Whether they are maximized or not, mere mortals cannot divine. Yet, without profits there can be (in the intermediate and long-term) no survival, and the firm will cease to exist. Profits are *sine qua non* if the firm is to retain access to capital, supplies of new materials, manpower, etc. in all except the very short-run.

While granting the importance of profit, the distinction between short and long-term profit maximization makes it easier to understand why many large enterprises act as though profit were not their primary objective. Consider the situation faced by Chrysler Corporation in 1979 and 1980. Quite clearly, many of its pricing and promotion decisions were motivated not by the desire for immediate profit, but by the objective of generating enough liquidity to enable the company to pay its bills and stay alive — even though this meant operating unprofitably for a considerable period. Faced with crisis then, large corporations with widely held shares seem less motivated by maximizing profit or shareholders' wealth than they are by the desire to survive. The nineteen-seventies witnessed many examples of companies for which net book values significantly exceeded market value, and yet their professional managements continued to fight for survival. Presumably, some of these managements might rationalize their actions in terms of an eventual return to profit (long-term, of course), but in the case of such long-running sagas as Pan Am or British Leyland, credulity would be stretched!

In our view, it should be clear from both a practical and theoretical perspective that profit is not the only objective for most large firms. Faced with crisis, the survival motive usually emerges as dominant, although we should recognize that as long as some element of competitiveness remains in the economic system, profits must at some point be made if the firm is to continue to survive as an independent entity. In this sense, we might view these objectives as hierarchically ordered, profits being the means by which the business enterprise perpetuates itself and, thus, survives.

How do these ideas jibe with the marketing concept, as we have explained it? To answer this question we must return to our distinction between immediate profit and longer-term profit. We said that deciding what to do in order to improve short-term profits was relatively easy, and in this sphere economics has given significant aid to the decision-maker. The job of the chief executive, however, is patently not merely to improve short-term profit, but rather to take actions which will ensure that the firm maximizes its stream of profits over the longer term — say three, five or ten years. This, we said, is an inordinately more difficult task. What should we do to ensure that we generate high profits over this period? What advice and guidance can be offered? It is precisely at this point that the marketing concept comes to the rescue. For while it would be clearly unrealistic to expect that we might give our chief executive detailed yet universal guidance to his job, the marketing concept comes just about as close to doing so as we might reasonably expect in this imperfect world.

What the marketing concept states so clearly is the essential task that must be performed if the firm is to make a profit: it must create customers. This is an absolutely necessary — if not sufficient — condition for any business enterprise. Customers are the only true asset possessed by any business firm. Its products and services may change, it may operate without employees as do many sole proprietorships, it may possess no unique technology nor capital resources, yet as long as it retains customers it can be a viable business. Without them, it is not.

Thus, we may view profits as a result of how well the customer creation and retention process is managed. If managed well, profits will result. If managed poorly, losses result. But without customers there can be no profit. Notice, then, that this is not a philosophy of "giving customers what they want" nor one which states that our sole purpose is to satisfy customer needs and desires. What it says is that creating and keeping customers is a necessary prerequisite for being profitable and surviving. The hierarchy of objectives in the marketing-oriented firm is thus as follows.

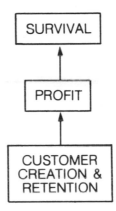

FIGURE 1-1 Hierarchy of Objectives

MARKETING AND THE CONTEMPORARY BUSINESS ENVIRONMENT

We noted that the need for a marketing orientation was seen in some companies more than twenty years ago. This need emerged as a consequence of changes taking place in the business environment that made it increasingly clear that customers would be in the driver's seat, so to speak. Since that time, the business environment has changed in such a way that more and more companies have been driven to adopt a similar perspective. We now briefly review some of these changes.

Inter-Industry Competition

For many companies, the major competitive threat to the achievement of their goals, if not to their very existence, is from competition which comes from outside their own industry, conventionally defined. To use Levitt's examples,[8] the major threats to the Hollywood movie companies came from television, not from each other, while the major threats to the railroads came from other forms of transportation — airlines for passengers and trucks combined with vastly improved highways for freight.

Clearly the phenomenon we are discussing is not new, but the years since Levitt wrote his classic article have witnessed a vast increase in inter-industry competition. In such diverse businesses as packaging, aircraft manufacture, watchmaking and automobiles, suppliers of different technologies and products compete vigorously for the same end use. To-day, however, the importance of this competitive phenomenon is greater than ever. Quite simply, many customers are basically indifferent about what technology is used to solve a problem, and they are often quite willing to change when a better alternative arrives.

In general, customers focus on function or need to be served, regardless of technology, so that their perspective on competing alternatives is more generic — a demand-based view of competition.[9] Manufacturers, since their competence is usually based upon technological factors, very often view competition in narrower terms — what has been called product-form competition[10] — which may sometimes create great strategic vulnerability to "outside" competition. Both the traditional slide rule manufacturers and watchmakers have suffered from the onslaught of the electronics companies, and some of Kodak and Fuji's conventional photographic products are already vulnerable to competing electronic alternatives such as videotape and disc.

International Competition

It takes little insight indeed to reach the conclusion that, more and more, we inhabit a global marketplace. The fifties, sixties and seventies witnessed tremendous growth of international competition spurred not only by successive GATT (General Agreement on Tariffs and Trade) rounds and the emergence of free trade areas of various types, but also by the kinds of economic strategies developed by Japan's Ministry of International Trade and Industry, or such countries as South Korea, Taiwan, Singapore, Brazil and so on. Even within the United States, long a bastion of economic independence — if not nationalism — foreign competitors have seized significant market shares in such industries as consumer electronics, automobiles, steel, tires, commercial banking and others. Today, whether from the perspective of the supply position or demand, no company can afford to view its business in solely domestic terms, and any which do so are, we venture to say, in peril.

Increased Product/Service Competition

A further characteristic of high-level economies, in particular, is the increased role of the service sector. The inevitable consequence is to lead to decreased market opportunities for product manufacturers. In modern society, examples are legion — and likely to increase as the economy continues to evolve. The family with two working spouses is likely to become even more service dependent in the future!

Examples of product-service competition exist in many industries but one internationally relevant example is the vast growth in travel, which has benefitted a great number of service industries, including hotels, restaurants, airlines, banks, insurance companies and others. Indeed, a marketing manager of one of Detroit's prestige cars once explained to me that he viewed the major threat to his business as European vacations! His point was that owners of the car he marketed might well decide to keep their car another year and take such a vacation, instead of trading it in on a new one. Such is the breadth of competition in an affluent economy.

Resource Scarcity

The shift in perceptions which OPEC (Organization of Petroleum Exporting Countries) has promoted is slowly bringing home to U.S. executives the fact that their country is no longer infinitely abundant in resources, and neither is the world. Thus, added to increased competition for customers' demand is increased competition for sources of labor, raw materials, components and even cash (supply). Japanese and European companies, in many cases blessed with less abundant resources, are sometimes more experienced in scouring the world for resources, but as U.S. supplies of crude oil and many ores become less available, so has the global quest for replacements heated up. Even marketing people should by now realize that a large share of market is of little consequence if the company loses its capability to supply and that we are competing for resources as well as access to customers and markets.

Removal of Regulatory Barriers to Competition

Although not yet a worldwide phenomenon, in Europe as well as the U.S., different regulatory attitudes have given signs of emerging — particularly in the late 1970's. Among U.S. industries which have been experiencing increased competition as a result of deregulation are telecommunications, banking, transportation (especially airlines), the traditional professions (especially doctors, dentists, optometrists and lawyers) and electronic media. Internationally, too, changes have taken place via the weakening of certain international cartels such as the International Air Transport Association (IATA), stronger antitrust enforcement (as has been emerging in the European Common Market) and changing government attitudes towards business, best exemplified by Margaret Thatcher in the United Kingdom.

We see the major reasons for this trend as lying in the poor economic performance of most of the free world's developed economies in the last part of the seventies. As a consequence, governments faced by the triple threat of inflation, slow growth and unemployment have been reexamining the basis of many of their regulatory policies in an attempt to seek greater economic efficiency. The general conclusion of such reexamination is that much regulation has impeded efficiency, reduced consumer welfare and generated a net cost to society which is sometimes considerable. As a result, the barriers have been coming down, the typical consequence being the discovery on the part of many previously-sheltered companies that they are ill equipped to deal with the vagaries of the truly competitive world. Of course, in certain areas the incursions of government regulation continue apace and little relief is likely in such areas as product liability, workplace safety, environmental pollution and the like. In the area of regulating market structure, however, some breathing space has been created.

Increased Pace of Market Development

Perhaps as a result of the changes we have been discussing, there is also little doubt that the pace at which markets are developing has speeded up very considerably. Greater scope of competition, more purchasing power, higher levels of literacy, more consumers and the growth of global markets have all had a dramatic influence. I was recently speaking to a business historian who pointed out that it took the sewing machine seventy-six years from introduction to reach its sales peak in the United States. Today, the sales of such major durables may be expected to peak in five to ten years or less. Clearly, there is less room for error, or even hesitation, in today's fast-moving markets.

Implications

If the marketing concept was helpful in the more competitive business environment that began to develop twenty or thirty years ago, it has become virtually essential today. It is now even more important to focus on changes in the external business environment, and to develop and offer products and services that will ensure that customers continue to prefer buying from us rather than our competitors.

SUMMARY AND CONCLUSIONS

In this chapter we have distinguished the marketing concept from other meanings of marketing, and described in general terms what it means to operate under this concept in a marketing-oriented firm. We have also explored the relationship between the marketing concept and the profit motive, and discussed the ongoing relevance of a marketing orientation to the contemporary business environment.

There can surely be little doubt about the competitiveness of the current business climate. Indeed, it might be argued that for marketing, these are the best of times and the worst of times. The best in the sense that the need for good marketing management and sound marketing strategy has probably never been greater. The worst because the business environment within which marketing managers are asked to deploy these skills is understandably difficult and challenging. The rewards for good marketing, however, are still there to be won, and we continue to believe that a true and wholehearted commitment to the practice of the marketing concept remains, in the long term, the best way to continue success and profitability. In Chapter 2, we develop this viewpoint further, by focussing upon the way in which decisions are made in the truly marketing-oriented firm.

REFERENCES AND FOOTNOTES

1 Robert J. Keith, "The Marketing Revolution," *Journal of Marketing*, Volume 24, No. 1, January, 1960, pp. 35-38.

2 *Ibid.*

3 *Ibid.*

4 *Ibid.*

5 *Ibid.*

6 Source: Keith, *op. cit.*

7 Herbert A. Simon, *The Sciences of the Artificial*, Cambridge, Mass.: M.I.T. Press, 1981, p. 52.

8 Theodore Levitt, "Marketing Myopia," *Harvard Business Review*, July-August, 1960, pp. 45-56.

9 George S. Day, Allan D. Shocker and Rajendra S. Srivastyava, "Consumer-Oriented Approaches to Identifying Product Markets," *Journal of Marketing*, Vol. 43, Fall 1979, pp. 8-19.

10 Philip Kotler, *Marketing Management: Analysis, Management and Control*, Englewood Cliffs, N.J.: Prentice Hall, 5th Edition, 1984, p. 83.

2

THE MARKETING-
ORIENTED FIRM

As we noted in the previous chapter, the marketing orientation is only one of many possible perspectives which the organization and its managers might adopt. Yet, despite the fact that its basic ideas were first articulated three decades ago, it remains both poorly understood and, even worse, poorly practiced. One of the major reasons for this phenomenon, we believe, is failure of marketing scholars and practitioners to make the idea really explicit. In Chapter 1 we defined the marketing concept and the marketing orientation. Yet it is all too easy to embrace (or pay lip service to) the concept without the faintest idea of how to put it into practice.

In this chapter we intend to redress this problem by making very clear what it means to operate with a marketing orientation. If a commitment to the marketing concept is to mean something it must, after all, have an impact on the kinds of decision that are made. It is upon decisions, and particularly resource allocation decisions, that we shall focus in the early part of the chapter.

The second part of the chapter has a different focus. We noted in Chapter 1 that there are a number of pitfalls which can beset a company attempting to shift to a marketing orientation. Thus, despite well-meaning and sincere commitments on the part of senior managers and others, the process of implementing the marketing concept can easily go astray. We have therefore devoted a good part of the chapter to discussing some of the common mistakes we have seen in attempts to adopt a marketing orientation.

DECISION MAKING IN A MARKETING-ORIENTED FIRM

What an individual manager views as being of primary importance affects how he or she evaluates alternatives and makes business decisions. The values which determine what is viewed as important obviously arise from a variety of sources. Some are no doubt influenced by past training and experience, others by the opinion of the boss or the culture of the current work organization and others, no doubt, by heredity. To operate under a marketing orientation, however, means that all of the diverse managers, functions and departments of the business enterprise must share a common commitment to the marketing concept: must not only share that commitment, but must act upon it when called to make the myriad decisions necessary to enable the organization to function. To use a current buzzword, the "corporate culture" must embrace this commitment very broadly if we are to be successful in adopting the marketing orientation.

To reiterate, the marketing-oriented firm operates with the philosophy that the creation and re-creation of customers is the central management task, as a necessary prerequisite for profits, growth and survival. This commitment to customers is not an end *per se*, but is a means to ensure its own long-term prosperity in a competitive market place. As a consequence of this commitment, the marketing-oriented firm operates differently from companies with other orientations. This we now examine, by reviewing some examples of the way in which decisions are made.

Pricing Decisions

The pricing decision is one in which there is a very clear distinction between firms operating with a marketing orientation and some other orientation. Most companies determine their selling prices by estimating cost, adding a desired profit margin, thereby arriving at a price (hence the label "cost plus"). Such an approach to pricing is anathema to the marketing-oriented firm, which recognizes that pricing must be based upon demand or what customers are willing to pay. Viewed from this perspective, it can easily be argued that target costs may be derived from the target selling price, rather than *vice versa*! Thus the way in which target prices are determined in a marketing-oriented firm is radically different from other companies. Pricing is, of course, a very complex topic, but we address it in a great deal more detail in Chapter 10.

Advertising and Promotion Decisions

Another good example of how decisions are made in marketing-oriented firms is provided by the way many firms make decisions about spending on marketing communications. For firms without a marketing orientation, such expenditures are often viewed, at best, as a necessary evil. They are expenditures to be minimized whenever possible, cut immediately when crisis threatens, and are sometimes regarded — particularly in technologically-oriented firms — as unproductive, diverting resources from the more important activity of technological development.

The contrast with a marketing-oriented firm is evident. Instead of being convinced that these expenditures are at best an unpleasant and excessive cost of doing business to be avoided whenever possible, marketing-oriented firms regard advertising and promotion expenditures as *investments* in the development of customers and markets. Such communications expenditures are viewed, then, as desirable and productive, with the recognition that by developing markets, these expenditures can produce long-term returns, like any other investment. Obviously, we are not arguing for increasing such expenditures *per se* — just pointing out the fundamental difference in attitude involved in the two kinds of firms.

Decisions on Gathering Marketing Information

Just as nonmarketing-oriented firms may approach their communications expenditures grudgingly, so are they typically unwilling to spend on market information — conventional marketing research, competitive intelligence and the like. There are many examples of this bias. Budgets for technological R&D, for example, are several orders of magnitude greater than those for market information for most manufacturers, yet research on causes of new product failure suggest time after time that inadequate market analysis and forecasting of customer and competitive response are often the reason for failure.[1] Research on the formation of multinational subsidiaries has also found that establishing a subsidiary marketing research function is often delayed despite the strategic importance of market information.[2] We should note here, however, that when we emphasize marketing information, we do not wish to imply generally the formality of a full-fledged marketing research department, but merely an openness toward and willingness to gather external market information. It is tragic that in many nonmarketing-oriented firms, only the costs of this kind of activity are considered — they fail completely to perceive the possible benefits.

Organized Product Development Process

A further sure indication of a company without any inkling of a marketing orientation is a complete lack of any organized process for the development of new products. Lacking a mechanism for identifying, screening and selecting development possibilities such companies are often forced into a pattern of imitative responses to the initiatives of others, with a record of declining margins and profitability. In a marketing-oriented company, development procedures are clearly established and communicated, and the organizational responsibilities for new product development are likewise unambiguous.

Customer Service Decisions

Attitude toward level and quality of customer service is a clear distinction between firms which operate with a marketing orientation and those which do not. Marketing-oriented companies recognize that their ability to win repeat customers depends upon assuring that customers remain satisfied with prior purchases. As a result, they place great emphasis upon the delivery of customer service, precluding the need for it wherever possible by high quality products, clearly communicated terms and —where appropriate—operating and/or installation support. When service is needed, however, it is prompt, of high quality, and delivered in a way that is sensitive to the importance of the customer.

Companies which lack the marketing orientation frequently fail to recognize the strategic importance of customer service. Spare parts manufacturing is scheduled at the company's convenience, often resulting in long delivery delays and costly downtime for customers. The organizational position of customer service is tucked away somewhere in a corner perhaps reporting to manufacturing or purchasing rather than to marketing or directly to general management. Service positions are not staffed by the most competent people. Field service representatives are often poorly educated and trained—and the whole activity is often underbudgeted, as well as being the first to be cut in crisis. Surely, that is no way to create and re-create customers! Contrast this with the philosophy of IBM, who have always believed that service was their business.

Breadth of Product Line

Many nonmarketing-oriented companies run a great danger of having inappropriate breadth of line — either too narrow or too broad. Production-oriented firms frequently end up with very narrow lines, which in the face of diverse customers needs, lead to worsening marketplace performance. Ford, with the Model T, and, to a lesser extent but more recently, Volkswagen, with the Beetle, provide examples of the narrow line and rigidity which often accompany a production orientation. Clearly, manufacturing economics are greatly improved by long runs of a limited variety of products, but if those products move into inventory and not out of it, then little has been gained!

On the other hand, sales-oriented and technologically oriented companies often end up with lines that are too broad, although for different reasons. In the case of sales-oriented firms, products proliferate because of the unwillingness to turn down any customer request, and the overwhelming desire for volume. In the technological case, the engineering interests of many managers may lead them to be enticed into solving a wider and wider variety of customer application problems, with consequent growth in the breadth of product line. A marketing-oriented company recognizes that it cannot meet the needs of all possible customers while generating the profits necessary to retain the ability to serve any customers in the future! It is crucial, then, to be selective about both the choice of customer targets and the choice of which of their needs the firm will attempt to satisfy. At the same time, however, we recognize that some variety is not only necessary, but desirable. Any color as long as it's black doesn't make it in today's competitive and sophisticated markets.

Planning and Budgeting Decisions

Many companies do not properly comprehend the purpose or process of planning and budgeting. First, in many such firms, there are no marketing plans. Indeed, even the distinction between plans and budgets may not be understood, such that the firm may believe it has a plan, when all that exists is a budget. (A necessary, though not sufficient distinction between the two is that the former is expressed in words, the latter in numbers!) In addition, many companies seem to believe that *the* purpose of planning is to develop a budget which then can be used for control purposes. They therefore fail to consider the other purposes of planning, thus compromising their potential for performance.

In a marketing-oriented firm, it is recognized that budgets are a derivative of the plan. They represent the financial implications of the plan in terms of costs, revenues and profits. Primary focus, however, is upon the development of the plan itself. Planning and budgeting are recognized to be interrelated activities, in which the financial implications of alternative strategies and courses of action are explored.

Dealing with Product Problems

When faced with the problem of a defective product, the gut reaction of many firms is to fight back — often legally — to minimize the short-term financial consequences. Such a reaction may be suicidal in the medium to long term, especially given the regulated, political and communications-rife world in which we live. By fighting their radial tire problems so hard, Firestone ended up courting disaster. Procter and Gamble, however, when they became aware of the toxic shock syndrome and its incidence among users of "Rely" tampons reacted almost immediately by withdrawing the product. The women of America, of course, constitute a market which is vitally important to P&G. They buy from P&G such items as detergents and other household cleaning products, food products, paper products, personal care products and so on. It would have been utter foolishness to have jeopardized these relationships by recalcitrance, and in their prompt response to the problem, Procter and Gamble provided an excellent example of the marketing-oriented firm at work.

Allocating under Scarcity

When a product is in short supply, the firm is faced with the decision of either raising the price or devising some allocation or rationing mechanism. If the shortage is to be temporary, as is inevitably the case, many companies are reluctant to raise price, and therefore choose the latter. The way in which a product is allocated, however, is instructive. In many companies, the product is sold to customers with the highest gross margin, and others are cut off. Another frequent approach is to cut back all customers by an equal proportion of their orders, sufficient to match the overall shortfall. Either approach is unacceptable to the marketing-oriented firm, the former by failing to consider the long-term profit potential of customer relationships, the latter because it produces the same result by treating customers unselectively. The marketing-orienting company recognizes the strategic importance of decisions about which commitments to fulfill, and makes the decision based on its long-term customer development objectives.

Quality of Forecasting

Many firms are trammelled by chronic revenue-forecasting errors. Unwillingness to invest in market information means they have a very superficial understanding of the demand dynamics of their market, and as a result their volume forecasts are notoriously poor. Though the result is normally to produce a series of operational problems including missed delivery dates, excessive inventories and high operating cost, they are often amazingly reluctant to invest the time and effort necessary to solve the problem, again because of their basic orientation. Marketing-oriented firms are distinguished by better forecasts and objectives which are more often met, a consequence of their superior knowledge of their market place.

Credit Extension

Most of the classic arguments about credit policy reflect disagreement over the liberality with which it is extended. Sales departments typically argue for loose guidelines to facilitate generation of sales volume, while controllers and financial officers, wary of collection problems, often err on the conservative side. Our concern here is less with the overall credit risk policy, however, than with the fact that such policies are often too rigid. Credit extension in a truly marketing-oriented firm is selective, with more generous facilities being granted to those customers upon whom the company has focused its long-term goals. This particular aspect of marketing has been well understood by bankers for years, but the blind adherence to rigid and unselective credit extension by their manufacturing and other clients still continues.

Response to Recession

Recession is an excellent time to build market position and secure a long-term relationship with customers. To achieve these goals the firm must have sufficient resources to withstand the downturns, but even with these resources nonmarketing-oriented firms frequently fail to grasp the opportunity because they are often too preoccupied with immediate financial results, as well as being insensitive to the competitive opportunities in their markets. In too many of these companies, the gut reaction is to cut back on advertising and promotion expenditures — a reaction which may seem somewhat paradoxical when the problem is lack of sufficient orders! Indeed, merely by cutting back less than its competitors, the firm may gain strategic advantage, for competitors who lose volume during recessions are usually more likely to ascribe the loss to the recession itself than to competitors' growing market share.

Strategies for Dealing with Competition

This final point is a key one. Part of a marketing orientation is enhanced openness to and awareness of the external environment, and that, of course, includes competition. For many firms, the existence of competition seems difficult for them to acknowledge. Whereas competitors' strategies play an important part in the planning and strategizing of a marketing-oriented firm, they are often ignored by other companies. In oligopolistic industries, the consequences of such attitudes can be catastrophic — and the U.S. steel, automobile and airframe companies have all made these kinds of errors in the post-World War II period. In marketing-oriented companies, there is a focus on how to beat the competition and, as we shall see in Chapter 6, this focus is an integral part of designing the marketing strategy.

MISUNDERSTANDING THE MARKETING ORIENTATION

There are many pitfalls for the unwary in attempting to become a more marketing-oriented company. Some of these arise because of the past traditions of the company and its managers, which become embodied in its culture. Others have their origins in the burst of sometimes naive enthusiasm that often accompanies first awareness of the importance of the marketing concept. Yet others result from regression to old patterns of behavior as the initial excitement of change loosens its grip. We now examine a number of these problems.

The Influence of Past Tradition

It is hard to underestimate the difficulties involved in attempting to change the orientation of a large, mature company. As we have commented, while the marketing orientation seems particularly timely and well-suited to today's very competitive environment, it is only one of many possible ways of orienting the firm. Some companies are still stuck firmly with the production orientation. In these companies, the heart of the business is the plant. Manufacturing managers are very powerful within the organization, and it is difficult to rise to top management by any other route. Profit centers are inevitably plant- rather than product- or market-based, and this reinforces the already strong tendency of manufacturing to "call the shots." The key to improving business performance is most usually seen as improving productivity and reducing cost, unfortunately too often without regard to customers' wishes with respect to product quality, delivery and service. In the U.S., this orientation is found among such companies as integrated steel producers and heavy engineering firms, although even in some of the more resistant quarters, changes are beginning to occur.

Among other companies — and particularly those working with commission reimbursement, such as insurance companies, brokerage firms and advertising agencies — a sales orientation is prevalent. Here the route to salvation is inevitably seen as increasing volume (billings). In the extreme, the salesforce and its wishes become the dominant influence on the firm. One of the major challenges faced by Merrill Lynch, the large U.S. financial services company, as it attempted to broaden its scope beyond mere brokerage, was to win the support and endorsement of its strategy from its numerous brokers. Under a sales orientation, control of prices, terms of sale and credit extension is inevitably loose, since to be otherwise would jeopardize the ability to expand volume. Further, because the focus is upon immediate and flexible response to today's customers' demands, there is usually little strategic thinking or development effort with respect to new products or new market entry. The net result is usually high volume with marginal profits, a situation which is quite common in the U.S. today.

Naturally, other orientations are possible. Mackay, for example, describes a technological and a financial orientation which are instantly recognizable to managers who work in these kinds of firms.[3] These orientations are summarized in Table 2-1.

The point of summarizing these orientations is, of course, to emphasize that it is important to know our starting point before we begin contemplating a shift of orientation. The traditions we are discussing become embedded in the firm's organization structure, its operating systems and its accounting systems—as well as in its managers' minds. Only when immediate and dire crisis threatens is it possible (perhaps) to win a broad consensus on the need for change, and even then it proves most difficult to execute. That it can be done is evidenced by such examples as Canon, which revolutionized the 35mm camera business in the 1970's, but generally, we must approach the process of change more gradually and piecemeal. Traditions often die hard.

TABLE 2-1   Technological and Financial Orientation[4]

Technological Orientation

- Emphasis is on research and engineering *per se*, with little recognition of economic considerations.
- Market criteria to guide research and development are inadequate or nonexistent.
- The product is considered the responsibility of the technical organization, with little product planning influence from marketing.
- There is a tendency to overengineer products to satisfy internal inclinations, or even whims, beyond what the customer needs or is willing to pay for.
- Basic development, product, and facility decisions are often made between engineering and manufacturing management, without marketing participation.

Financial Orientation

- The emphasis tends to be on short-range profit at the expense of growth and longer-range profit.
- Budgeting and forecasting frequently preempt business planning.
- Efficiency may outrank effectiveness as a management criterion.
- Pricing, cost, credit, service, and other policies may be based on false economy influences and lack of marketplace realism.
- The business focus is not on the customer and market but on internal considerations and the numbers.

Manufacturers' Problem

It should not be difficult to envisage the major orientation difficulties faced by manufacturers. Their core strengths, typically, have been in research, engineering or manufacturing. These were the skills which generally gave rise to the company and provided its *raison d'être*, its organizing force. Most of the key management of the company in its early days — and, often, still today — came from these functions, and as a result there is a general tendency to enshrine the virtues of these functions or disciplines at the expense of others.

Yet, for the manufacturing company to survive and prosper, it must find and develop markets for its products. As we have noted, customers are central to the operation of any business — even a manufacturing business! As a result, manufacturers must lead away from their core strengths if they wish to be successful. It is not enough for them to excel at research, development or manufacturing; they must also do a reasonably competent job of marketing if they are to reap any economic gain for their efforts. This is not an easy task and to be a good marketing manager in such an organization demands a very high level of professional commitment, for a whole combination of forces are conspiring to enforce the company-dominated view to the virtual exclusion of the customer, a bias which, if it is to be redressed, demands a high level of both emotional strength and intellectual competence.

The Retail and Distribution Problem

If manufacturers have a typical paucity of customer orientation, then retail and distribution businesses often suffer from excess. The danger is that those close to the customer, such as specialized buyers, department managers or store managers, may become so oriented toward their customer that they neglect the needs of the company itself. These patterns of behavior we would construe as manifestations of a sales orientation rather than a marketing orientation, but evidence of their existence would show up in the following ways: excessively broad merchandise line, slow turnover on many items in the line, very slow receivables turnover, poor credit record, excessive returns and so on. In our opinion these are *not* the major reasons why so many large U.S. retailers experienced difficult times in the 1970's, but they are problems against which most retail businesses must be continuously vigilant, since they derive directly from their basic strengths and competencies in dealing with customers.

Residual Supply Orientation

It is quite evident that the job of marketing is much easier under conditions of excess demand. Indeed, some would argue that there is little need for marketing in such a situation. In contrast, marketing in really competitive markets is a difficult, risky, complex job. Little wonder then, that there lurks in the hearts of many managers a reluctance to accept the competitive imperative. Their wishful thinking is to be able to dominate their markets by divining whom and at what price they will supply. To maintain such attitudes within a marketing department, faced with the realities of the marketplace, is difficult — but in other functions, more removed from the competitive cut-and-thrust, it is much easier. We have met the enemy and it is us, is the situation in some companies — which are characterized by a variety of interrelated syndromes, such as:

"NIH"	— if it's not invented here, it's no good.
"We're the greatest"	— a sincerely-held belief that in every area the company excels.
"The only news is good news"	— a rejection of any evidence which suggests that the company is not doing well.

Clearly, in the extreme, such attitudes represent organizational pathology. However, a smattering of these beliefs survives in most companies, and acts as a real impediment to a true marketing orientation. Openness to the environment, to information generated outside the company, is a hallmark of a marketing-oriented company, and creating and maintaining this attitude is one of the key challenges for marketing management.

The Dangers of Overreaction

Another class of problems which crop up in attempting to implement a marketing orientation are those that result from failing to get the customer orientation into proper perspective. One typical syndrome we call the omniscient customer, while another results from elevating the customers' wishes to the level of an imperial command, which we call the omnipotent customer.

The Customer Omniscient

A common mistake, particularly in the early stages of attempting to become customer-oriented, is to believe that customers are the source of all wisdom. Not so! It is a mistake (generally) to believe that customers can design products, forecast their own sales levels precisely, tell you exactly what they will need three, four or five years from now and so on. Customers have no monopoly on foresight, and usually have analogous traditions, habits or policies to those of their suppliers. What is key, however, is to recognize that whatever the customer does think, right or wrong, subjective though it may be, is a vital part of the reality with which the firm must deal. Should it be reluctant to do so, it will increase its competitive vulnerability to any supplier which appreciates the importance of customer opinions. Further, we should learn to be selective in the way in which we respond to such customer inputs, for among most companies' customer bases there are indeed some who *can* design products, give help in forecasting sales or in divining the future of their industry. Customers are not omniscient, but they are important, and some can be very helpful.

The Customer Omnipotent

A similarly unrealistic response to attempting to develop a marketing orientation is what we call the customer omnipotent. In this scenario, the response to the marketing concept is to attempt to provide the customer with everything he wants. A moment's pause for reflection will quickly demonstrate the futility of this approach. If we assume profit or utility maximization to be the goal of all the buyers, then clearly in any transaction they will be motivated to seek the maximum number of advantages — including being paid to take the product or service we offer! Indeed, to act this way is to practice more of a sales orientation than a marketing orientation.

Perhaps we should now reemphasize the point that there is nothing altruistic about the marketing concept. Quite simply, customers do not work for our company — they have different interests and objectives. The marketing-oriented firm's commitment to customers does *not* grow out of any desire to maximize customer welfare (although this may be the result) but out of the pragmatic, hard-nosed quest to find a rationale which will produce high quality long-term profits and growth in a complex, fast-changing and very competitive environment. It should therefore be clearly recognized that customers are not omnipotent, nor can we afford to let them be, since they do not (in general) have our interests at heart. Equally clear, however, is the fact that they must always remain a potent influence on the firm, or its prospects will dim.

Other Problems of Implementation

There is a miscellany of other impediments to developing a marketing orientation. Two we run across quite frequently, however, are halfhearted or superficial approaches to the problem.

Halfhearted Commitments

To damn with faint praise is a well-recognized part of many organizations' politics. Perhaps it is not always recognized, though, how often marketing efforts are condemned in a similar manner. Thus, many companies *talk* marketing orientation, but *shirk* applying it. They pay lip service to the importance of customer service — but operate with abysmal service levels; they avow the need for marketing research but find a market research expenditure of a few thousand dollars "unjustified" and so on. In our view, many companies practice pseudo-marketing. They are enamored of the glamor, the techniques of marketing, but lack that fundamental commitment to customers which characterizes the true marketing orientation. They do what they believe to be minimally necessary, not what they should recognize to be desirable.

Superficial Marketing

Superficial marketing may often be very sincerely motivated but nonetheless it is condemned to fail. Superficial marketing is basically short-term oriented. Instead of pausing to take stock of the long-term trends which will shape future customer needs, the focus is on the short-term, the quick fix which will produce immediate results but will compromise the longer-term position of the company.

There is a variety of factors which conspire to produce this superficial response to customers — of attending to their immediate wants at the expense of what will be their longer-term demands. One is inertia. The most difficult challenge for marketing management is to get their own organizations to adapt to the changes they see coming down the road. In the U.S., however, two other factors also accentuate the superficial response. One is the strong influence of the market price of their common stock on top management's time horizon. They are too often preoccupied with maintaining quarter-to-quarter gains in earnings per share regardless of what the long-term consequences for their company might be. If these short-term earnings gains can be supported without compromising the company's long-term future, all is well and good. But sometimes there is an unwillingness to batten down the hatches, cut back dividends and take the hard decisions on plant and equipment that may eventually be necessitated by impending crisis.

Yet another U.S. influence is the short time which U.S. managers spend in a given management job. America's individualist ethic demands frequent feedback, evidence of recognition and progress. This has traditionally taken the form of either fairly rapid promotion or transfer. A survey of consumer brand managers found they spent an average of only fourteen months on a given brand.[5] Little chance of long-term planning from these managers! Their concern is quite clearly with the short-term wants of their customers, and the prospects of a true marketing orientation are thereby dimmed.

SUMMARY AND CONCLUSIONS

In this chapter we have attempted to clarify what it really means to operate with a marketing orientation. We did this by examining a variety of possible orientations toward the business. We have also explored in depth what a truly marketing-oriented firm is *via* an explanation of how it makes certain key decisions. We have also tried to show how many companies misunderstand the marketing concept, whether through sincere mistakes or through deep-seated unwillingness to change their *modus operandi*.

The attitudes we discussed under the different orientations can, of course, persist in different departments or functions within the firm. What should be made clear, however, is that we are referring to orientations of the *whole company*. In this respect, it is perhaps unfortunate that the same label of "marketing" is usually applied to the concept and orientation, as is applied to the department. This can needlessly raise the hackles of managers working in departments other than the marketing department, who then oppose a shift to the marketing orientation because it is seen as a departmental power grab. For exactly this reason, one of our colleagues prefers to talk of customer orientation, while another uses the term "outward orientation" to convey the idea of an organization open to its environment, with respect to customer inputs, competitor information and the like.

Having concentrated to this point upon the importance of marketing to the company as a whole, however, we now shift our focus. In Chapter 3, we turn to the marketing department or function, examining what its role should be within the firm.

REFERENCES AND FOOTNOTES

1. Robert G. Cooper, "Dimensions of Industrial New Product Success and Failure," *Journal of Marketing*, Vol. 43, Summer 1979, pp. 93-103.
2. James M. Hulbert and William K. Brandt, *Managing the Multinational Subsidiary*, New York: Holt, Rinehart and Winston, 1980.
3. From Edward S. Mackay, *The Marketing Mystique*, New York: American Management Association, 1972.
4. *Ibid.*, pp. 18-19.
5. Steven R. Palesy, *A Behavioral Theory of Product Manager Motivation and Performance*, Unpublished Ph.D. Dissertation, New York: Columbia University, 1977.

THE JOB
OF MARKETING

In this chapter, we turn for the first time to the marketing function or department within the firm. Our goal is the define the job which the chief executive should expect his marketing department to perform for him. In defining the job which should be done, we shall also comment upon the way the job normally gets done, and some of the problems which arise. We hold strongly to the view that the responsibilities and tasks of marketing must be defined from the perspective of markets. In most organizations, and particularly in manufacturing organizations, there is usually an excess of persons capable of thinking in terms of products, technologies, programs, departments, etc. — but a terrible shortage of people whose orientation is market-and-customer-based. Marketing is the sole function of the business enterprise whose charge is thusly based, and to neglect this basic concept is to be most fundamentally delinquent.

In addition to developing the basic requirements of the marketing job, we shall also illustrate how those requirements should be met by examining the basic principles of analysis that underlie the development of competitive marketing strategies. Finally, we summarize the relationship between the job's requirements and its principle activities, and discuss the implications for companies' marketing actions.

THE RESPONSIBILITIES OF MARKETING MANAGEMENT

As Figure 3-1 indicates, there are three key responsibilities of marketing management. Each will now be examined.

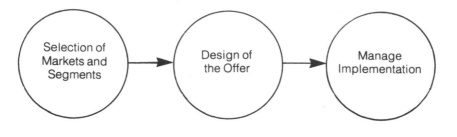

FIGURE 3-1 Responsibilities of Marketing Management

Selection of Markets and Segments

The first and foremost responsibility of marketing is to recommend in which markets and which segments of markets the firm should be competing. Except for those which are very new, all markets consist of segments — groupings of customers seeking similar things (to be more rigorously defined later) — and one of the most important decisions for the firm is to decide in which of these segments it will compete. This choice — sometimes called strategic segmentation — is usually a general management decision and is not normally made by marketing managers. Rather, they should perform the necessary information collection, analysis and interpretation such that the general manager or Chief Executive Officer can make a good choice. In other words, this is a key role for marketing — but one in which it typically acts in an advisory capacity, making recommendations to top management.

In Figure 3-2 we illustrate the fact that there is a hierarchy of market selection involved. At the broadest and most general level are the choice of industry and market, both of which are typically strategic for the corporation as a whole, and for its individual divisions or businesses. It is important to recognize that these are key strategic decisions, for they represent major investment allocation decisions among competing marketing opportunities. Recalling our discussion of the marketing-oriented firm, they are arguably the most important decisions made in the firm. If not the most important, choice of market certainly ranks along with choice of technologies and products as among the most important. A vice president of U.S. Steel once put this decision into perspective in a telling and succinct manner when he said, when trying to explain marketing, "Which would you rather own, a plant or a market?" Little doubt, surely, which most firms would like to own — but it is a much more difficult undertaking to own a market than it is to own a plant.

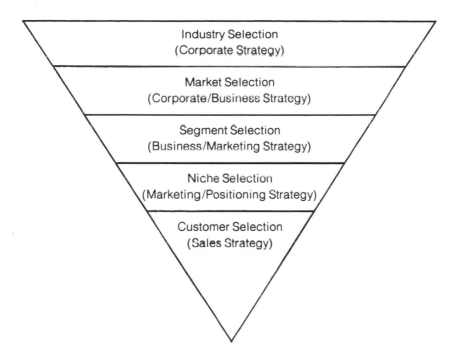

Industry Selection
(Corporate Strategy)

Market Selection
(Corporate/Business Strategy)

Segment Selection
(Business/Marketing Strategy)

Niche Selection
(Marketing/Positioning Strategy)

Customer Selection
(Sales Strategy)

FIGURE 3-2 The Market Selectivity Hierarchy

The process of selecting markets and customers does not cease with choice of industry and market, however. As we noted, these decisions typically lie within the domain of the CEO or Division President. The next two choices are typically the focus of the marketing strategy, and these entail deciding upon the segment(s) of the overall market which the firm will pursue, and its positioning within segment(s) — i.e. which particular niche it will seek to carve out for itself. These particular choices will be examined in more detail later in the chapter.

Process of Market Selection

The process of market selection requires the collection and analysis of a variety of information. Note, however, that the focus of this information should be on the future, not the present or the past. Relevant information may be grouped into the following categories, with some suggested questions.

Customers	What will customers in these markets be wanting in the future?
	How many of them will there be?
	What will be their purchasing power, willingness to buy?
Competitors	Who will be competing for these customers or needs?
	What will they be offering these customers?
	What results will they be seeking in return for meeting these needs?
Technology	What will be the kinds of products/services/technologies capable of meeting (or substituting for) these needs?
	What will be the timing of key technological developments?
	Who is sponsoring them?
	What is the future cost-competitiveness of relevant systems?
	What are the implications for our current products/services and technologies?
Government	What is expected future course of government regulation in this market?
	How will it affect us?
	How might it change the nature of competition in this industry?
Resources	What is the supply outlook for key resources?
	Is there a likelihood of cartelization of supply?
	Are competitors integrating backwards?
Company Capabilities	What is the strength of the company's total capital structure — can it finance this alternative?
	What competence does the company possess in this type of market?

Quite clearly, it is simply impossible to scan all possible markets and segments with the depth necessary for sound strategy development. This is where the mission statement that defines the business (Chapter 5) plays a key role, by focussing the attention of marketing management into defined areas. Thus, corporate and business strategies should provide guidance in terms of which general market opportunity areas should come within the purview of marketing's search.

Design of the Offer

The second key mandate to marketing must be the job of designing the offer that will be made to the segments that have been selected. In the typical market, as we have remarked, this means coming to grips with the wants and needs of particular market segments, and developing a package of values or benefits which meets those needs or wants. In this aspect, the role of marketing is seen as a type of engineering activity, but the design which marketing develops must be more comprehensive than just the product or service itself. The key concept with which marketing must work in designing an offer which is to be brought to market is that of the "marketing mix," defined by Jerome McCarthy as the four "P's," Product, Price, Place and Promotion,[1] but here viewed a little differently. Figure 3-3 depicts the five major components of the marketing mix as we define them, *viz.* product, price, distribution, service and promotion. Figure 3-3 also shows some of the ways in which each element might be varied.

Although only relatively few examples of variation are shown below, they should suffice to make a point: there are literally millions of alternative marketing mixes available in a given market, so that there is no reason for one company's offer to be identical to another's, except by design (imitation strategy). Agreed, some of the theoretically feasible mixes may be practically impossible, while the possibles vary greatly in their desirability and profit potential — but the basic point remains; except for deliberately imitative strategies, it is only lack of imagination and capability which results in identical or near-identical offers. The major corollary, of course, is that there should be no such thing as a "commodity" product in a company where marketing is doing its job. We shall return to this point later in the chapter.

The second responsibility of marketing, then, is to use the tools which comprise the marketing mix to design an offer which can meet the needs of customers thus creating value and benefit for those customers.

Manage Implementation

The last key responsibility of marketing management is to manage implementation of the chosen design or strategy. Note that wherever the first two responsibilities we have discussed are strategic in nature, the last is primarily concerned with the operating responsibility of marketing managers. There are, however, two aspect to managing implementation.

The first involves securing the commitment of other functions and departments to the design (strategy) which has been developed. In Chapter 6, we shall examine in more detail this issue of coordination or integration- — suffice it to say it is this point that is vital. The other aspect of implementation is also important, for it involves managing the offer in the marketplace; fine-tuning the strategy, modifying the tactics, trading off objectives (see Chapter 6) and so on. Much of this activity is directly performed by others

34

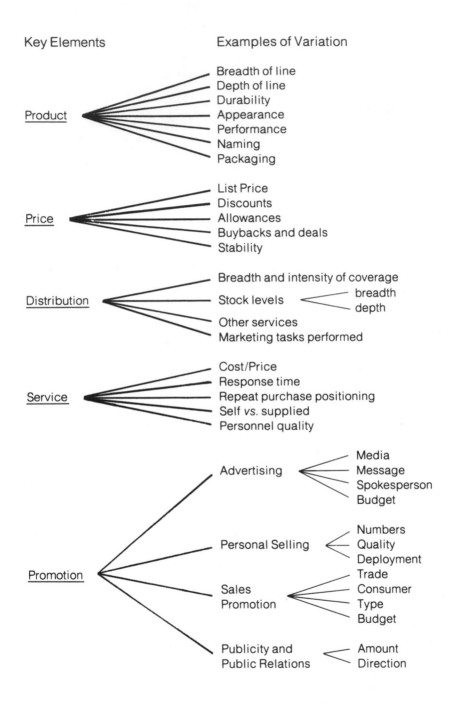

FIGURE 3-3 Marketing Mix

—notably the field salesforce, promotion experts, advertising agencies, etc.—but the overall responsibility lies with marketing.

We now return to the first aspect of implementation, really achieving interfunctional coordination. This can pose many problems in organizations with poor internal working relationships, or when marketing management lacks the necessary interpersonal skills. It is often alleged that Japanese companies have superior capabilities in achieving such coordination, and that these have greatly aided their ability to compete with Western companies. Too many European and U.S. competitors seem hampered by interdepartmental strife and rivalry, such that precious management time is mistakenly redirected from dealing with external threat and opportunity to dealing with internal conflict.

Given that we have solved the immediate problem of gaining commitment, however, the business of managing the offer still poses important problems. Here we find too often that antiquated—or, at least, no longer appropriate—management systems are the villain of the piece. While it is true that many other factors—such as wrong organization, poor management or even competitive brilliance—may yet stymie our plans, a necessary (though perhaps not sufficient) condition for success must be to ensure that such systems for compensation, planning, objective-setting, etc., are in line with the strategies we are pursuing. Volume-based salesforce compensation systems, for example, tend to work well while there are plenty of growth opportunities—but may lead to great dissatisfaction in declining markets. Similarly, ratchet-like quota systems are better suited to growth products than to those in maturity or decline.

By far the most serious problems of this type, however, are a direct result of planning systems that are seriously out of kilter. The most common and very dangerous problem is the lack of consistency in the timing of various contributions to the planning effort. Remembering that the scope of marketing encompasses such activities as advertising, promotion and personal selling, it should be evident that the key elements of the marketing strategy and plan must be in place before coordinated sales, advertising, promotion or distribution plans can be developed. Nonetheless, in many companies these activities remain either unplanned, are planned out of sequence, or even developed independently, such that chances of successful implementation are virtually zero. We shall return to this theme several times, both later in the chapter as well as later in the book, but it is clearly central to the issue of coordination.

PRINCIPLES OF MARKETING STRATEGY

The responsibilities of marketing management are, of course, important to an understanding of the role of the marketing department within the firm. Of more interest to the strategist, however, is how managers should go about executing those responsibilities. There are three principles which are basic to the successful execution of the marketing job, and these three underlie almost all successful marketing strategies. We shall now examine each of them.

The Principle of Selectivity and Concentration

As we have noted, the selection of markets and segments is one of the primary responsibilities of marketing. The process of doing so involves gathering a considerable amount of information, and the use of a variety of screening rules, often incorporated in a series of strategy statements (See Chapters 4, 5, and 6). In the decision process, however, is a very basic principle of marketing strategy, which we call the principle of selectivity and concentration. This principle, of course, is not only central to the development of marketing strategy, but lies at the heart of all good strategy. Military literature abounds with prescriptions supporting this principle. Napoleon, for example, stated that the secret of strategy is the concentration of firepower on the right battlefield. Von Clausewitz suggested the heart of all strategy is the concentration of strength, while Liddell-Hart augmented this view to emphasize the concentration of strength against enemy (competitor) weakness.

There are two aspects to the principle of selectivity and concentation. The first demands that the marketing manager must carefully select the market target, the second mandates concentration of resources against that target. We now concentrate on the first aspect.

Selectivity is widely preached and sometimes even practiced in marketing. The best-known manifestation of this principle is in market segmentation. However, we find segmentation so widely misunderstood and poorly applied, that we remain skeptical of the achievement of sufficient selectivity in marketing strategy.

Let us begin by defining a market segment. A segment is constituted by a grouping of actual or potential customers which will respond in a similar way to a given offer. Note that from a pragmatic perspective, it is the difference in response that is key. However, to develop insight into segmentation, we must ask *why* they respond differently. The answer lies in the benefits that customers are seeking, and the priorities they place upon satisfaction of those benefits. This difference in customer wishes, then, underlies all segmentation, no matter how apparently sophisticated the statistical methods or model used in segmentation research. Indeed, the more erudite the methodologies involve, the more important it becomes to keep this point in mind. As Figure 3-4 shows, the ultimate "segmentation" takes the form of making to individual order. Since individuals differ, so —

in an ultimate sense — do their wants and desires, thus individuation is optimal for consumer satisfaction. Unfortunately, however, the economics of production are usually in conflict with the economics of consumption on this point, for custom production is usually very expensive, and the result is the attempt at compromise which is constituted by market segmentation.

The fundamental basis by which markets are segmented, then, is by customers needs or wants, or, alternatively viewed, by customer problem or benefits sought. There are, therefore, two parts to a segmentation study. The first consists of describing the benefit (problem) structure of the marketplace and a variety of increasingly sophisticated techniques are available to assist in this process. The second part involves identifying the types of customers who seek the various kinds of benefits or to solve particular kinds of problems. In this latter role of identification, traditional demographic measures are most often used, but other more elaborate schemes involving in addition more psychological responses (psychographics) are now quite often employed in consumer markets.

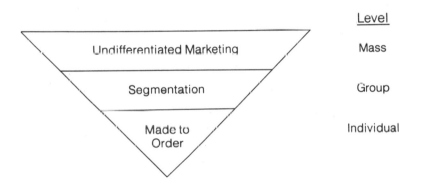

FIGURE 3-4 The Hierarchy of Segmentation

Segmentation has occupied a venerable slot in the literature of marketing for many years now. However, it is only fair to point out that by far the majority of this literature focusses on methods of performing segmentation studies. Interesting as it may be, from a strategy perspective, the key issues revolve around what to do with such information once gathered. While better descriptive understanding of a market may ultimately *permit* better strategy decisions, it by no means *guarantees* the same. The issue of choosing segments or niches, then, is the central strategy issue. Here the second part of our principle comes into play — namely, concentration of resources.

No organization, no matter how large, is possessed of infinite resources. The Japanese have always been conscious of resource limitations, for such are embedded in their culture and life style. In other parts of the world, however, and particularly in the United States, resources have sometimes been used profligately, a practice admittedly often encouraged by government policy. Today, however, resource constraints are recognized almost universally. In government and industry, the attitude epitomized in the saying, "Throw enough money at a problem and it will go away" has withered rapidly. Economics, of course, is the social science concerned with the problem of allocating scarce resources, and there is well-developed literature on the subject. Here, however, we focus on one key issue, namely, the danger of attempting too much, thereby dissipating the impact of limited resources by spreading them over too many alternatives. To gain strategic advantage demands concentration of resources whether for the large firm or the small. Indeed, many large companies frequently experience their most difficult competitive problems with smaller firms which have focused their resources on a particular segement of the market. This concentration enables "small fry" to attain more leverage with their slender resources than some of their larger competitors which spread their resources thinly. Some classic examples are present in the automotive industry, where firms like Chrysler and British Leyland have had their backs against the wall while BMW has prospered.

Notice that there are risks associated with a policy of concentration. Certainly some options which might have proved attractive will be rejected while others will be mistakenly chosen. However, to assume that a hedging approach of allocating a small amount of resources to all feasible options will reduce risk is fallacious. Indeed, in competitive markets it will often guarantee failure. How then shall we select segments and concentrate resources against them in a way which yields the results we seek? The answer lies in the next principle we shall discuss, the principle of differential advantage.

The Principle of Differential Advantage

The principle of differential advantage not only lies at the core of every successful strategy, it also is central to understanding what the job of the marketing manager is about. While sometimes masquerading under other labels, such as competitive advantage or edge, the same basic concept is key, and we will now examine its components.

The principle of differential advantage asserts — in simple terms — that the way to make high profits is to offer to customers something which they vant that they cannot get elsewhere. In other words, to use the marketing mix to design an offer that provides an economically justified group of customers with benefits which they are seeking, but which are not provided by the competition.

A number of different implications flow from this basic concept. First, it emphasizes the competitive nature of the business. Simply attempting to meet customer needs at a profit (one oft-invoked description of marketing) is not enough to promote our interests, for competitive parity may still result. We have to do it better or differently *in ways important to the customer* for our long-term gain. Second, it should be clear that some differentials are inherently better than others, the judgment (*ceteris paribus*) being dependent upon susceptibility to competitive imitation. It is perhaps for this reason, as well as tangibility, that so many manufacturers favor a differential based on the product element of the marketing mix, although other elements may be no more or even less liable to easy competitive imitation. Third, however, it is important to recognize that no matter how secure (protected by patent or otherwise) a differential advantage may appear to be, its eventual demise is inevitable in a competitive marketplace. Consequently, the marketing manager must recognize that the maintenance of a differential advantage is his primary job, and his search should be constant and continuing. Finally, we should also note not that all differences result in advantage—the world is littered with efforts that were truly different—but failed. The essential point is that those differences in the offer must create benefits *which are truly valued by our target customer* before an advantage can result.

The Principle of Integration

Our final principle is one upon which the success or failure of all the efforts discussed to date must rest. Very simply, it states that to assure the success of a strategy, its elements — both in design and execution — must be carefully integrated and coordinated. The chain analogy is a good one for marketing management, for just as a chain is only as strong as its weakest link, so is a marketing strategy only as strong as its weakest element. Poor advertising can damn an otherwise good product, delayed promotional materials can condemn a launch to failure, mispricing can cause havoc to sales forecasts and so on.

While almost *every* executive would agree in principle with the need for a carefully integrated plan and strategy, however, achieving such integration in practice is fraught with difficulty. As we noted earlier, one problem which may arise is the orientation of the firm. In designing an offer and developing a differential advantage, the firm is going about a task of benefit creation and delivery. The customer who seeks those benefits agrees to exchange money for them and, in theory, both participants in the transaction will then be better off.

The benefits then are the basis of the "contract" between buyer and seller, and the seller is thus in a position of making promises to the buyer. Promises because, even for nondurables, benefits are rarely enjoyed immediately upon exchange. Even though the seller often receives payment immediately, the customer enjoys the benefits at some point in the future. The seller therefore promises future benefit to the buyer, and the strategy in which the differential advantage is embedded (see Chapter 6) is a way of formalizing those promises. If those future benefits are not received by customers, it is evident that longer term prospects for the firm are limited. This simple argument may seem no more than a straightforward restatement and development of the marketing concept. Note, however, that while its logic may seem inescapable and even desirable to a marketing-oriented firm, a company with an orientation toward production or finance may well fail to recognize the centrality of these promises to the firm's future success. As a result, even where an integrated approach to the marketplace is initially developed, disintegration subsequently sets in as the firm reneges on its promises to customers via such actions as reduced service levels, withdrawal of support, excessive disputing of well-founded customer complaints and so on.

More typical than the above, however, is the situation where integration is never successfully achieved. Different functions or departments squabble over priorities, and the result is a mishmash of an offer, or one so diluted by the politics of coalitions that, yet again, an integrated package of benefits does not result.

To achieve integration requires agreement on priorities. As we shall see in Chapter 6, design of strategy is a highly constrained problem, and once agreement on the key elements of the differential advantage is reached, many other elements of the offer must fall into line within very narrow borders. Once this is achieved, we must determine that management systems (especially, but not exclusively, planning systems), organization

Responsibility	Principle
Selection of Markets and Segments	Selectivity and Concentration
Design the Offer	Differential Advantage
Manage Implementation	Integration

FIGURE 3-5 Relationship Between Responsibilities and Principles

structure and actions are such as to ensure the successful implementation of the integrated design. There is a tremendous amount of detailed planning which must go on to assure marketplace success. Yet it is this detailed planning which sets the direction and timing of marketing actions, which are, in the final analysis, the only concrete manifestation of marketing strategies and plans.

SUMMARY AND CONCLUSIONS

In this chapter we have reviewed the job of the marketing manager. We have argued that three tasks or responsibilities describe the job. The first is the selection of the markets and market segments in which the firm should do business — a responsibility typically discharged *via* an advisory role to the Chief Executive Officer. The second involves the design of the offer which is to be made to customers in these selected segments. Here the marketing manager should play a lead role in what is admittedly a complex task involving the commitment and cooperation of many different functions or departments. Both of these first two tasks are essentially strategic in nature. Finally comes the operating part of the marketing job which is to manage the process of implementing the offer, the job which takes much of the marketing manager's time, sometimes leading to the neglect of the first two tasks.

To execute these tasks well is a difficult assignment, but much facilitated by adherence to three basic principles of marketing strategy. The first of these is the principle of selectivity and concentration, which suggests the desirability of carefully and precisely selecting target market segments, then concentrating resources against those selected targets. The second principle — that of differential advantage — suggests that offers should be designed in such a way as to offer prospective customers benefits which they are really concerned about, but cannot find in competitors' offers. While difficult to fulfill, in this principle lies a recipe for great business success. Finally, we emphasized the principle of integration — the need to ensure that the different elements comprising the marketing strategy be carefully designed and implemented in a coordinated way. By whatever means, the marketing manager must find a way to achieve such integration — both within and outside marketing — or his efforts are doomed. We shall return to this subject in more depth in Chapter 6.

There is, of course, a relationship between the responsibilities we have defined and the principles of marketing strategy, a relationship which is depicted in Figure 3-5. By working with this perspective, it is possible for marketing management to play the stimulating and strategic role which is required if the firm is to prosper in these competitive times. The role requires an external and future-oriented attitude on the part of marketing managers, as well as a better understanding of the responsibilities of marketing on the part of general management. We turn to the role of marketing at the corporate level in the next chapter.

REFERENCES AND FOOTNOTES

1. E. Jerome McCarthy, *Basic Marketing: A Managerial Approach*, Homewood, Illinois: Richard D. Irwin, 6th Edition, 1978, p. 39.

4

MARKETING AND CORPORATE STRATEGY

We began this book by emphasizing the importance of the marketing concept to the company as a whole. The orientation toward customers and its impact on decision-making can have far-reaching effects on the firm and its performance. Marketing inputs are crucial in a different way, however, to the formulation of corporate strategy, and it is on this subject that we focus in this chapter. We begin by exploring the key decisions involved in corporate strategy, and then discuss how the criteria used to make these decisions have evolved over time. We next expand these changes into a review of portfolio approaches to key investment decisions, illustrating the different approaches developed by a variety of companies. We conclude by attempting to place the development of portfolio-based models into perspective, in terms of their advantages and disadvantages for management.

CORPORATE STRATEGY

We do not attempt to describe all the aspects of formulating corporate strategy in this chapter. Instead we concentrate on some key aspects. Strategies deal with major resource allocation decisions, and at the corporate level we are describing — for the most part — a process of choosing among alternative investment opportunities. This view of the corporate function as a capital-rationer is not, of course, new. Yet it is abundantly clear that the problem in a corporate context is somewhat different from the portfolio issues facing an individual investor, and, furthermore, that the way in which corporate management goes about identifying, assessing, and investing in alternative opportunities can have a profound effect on firm performance.

A particularly useful way to conceive of the investment alternatives facing corporate management is in terms of a matrix of products and markets. Thus, some of the most crucial corporate strategy decisions revolve around making investments in some products (technologies) *versus* others, and some markets (customers) *versus* others. This concept is reflected in Ansoff's approach to corporate strategy, for example, in terms of his four-box model,[1] *viz.*

	Present Products	New Products
Present Markets	Market Penetration	Product Development
New Markets	Market Development	Diversification

and has been incorporated in various ways by many other authors. Brion, for example, describes a nine-box extension of Ansoff's approach, as now used by a number of companies.[2]

One way to describe the corporation's portfolio of businesses, then, is in terms of occupancy of various cells in an extended product market matrix, as depicted below.

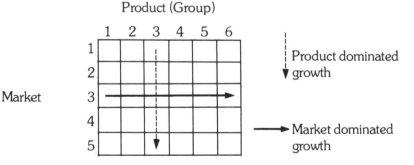

Most companies — and notably those we today call multinational — choose one primary growth direction and pursue it for as long as it seems fruitful. Multinational manufacturers, for example, have taken a product or group of products around the globe, seeking new markets. They have followed a product-dominated growth pattern, which would appear as a vertical arrow in the matrix above. As new markets for existing products become progressively more difficult to find, so have many international companies — such as Gillette and Honda — begun to look to new technologies and new products to further their growth. Other companies — particularly retailers — grow quite differently, however, typically using a market-dominated approach, augmenting and expanding their product mix as they seek to grow.

At this point we do not intend to advocate any one growth direction — yet it is very clear that the growth pattern which the firm follows across product/market cell boundaries is important. Rumelt's research suggests that companies which expanded by maintaining some degree of "relatedness" in their businesses — for example, by products (technologies) or markets (customers) — were typically more profitable than those which diversified in an unrelated manner — a purely conglomerate form.[3] Such gradual or evolutionary diversification moves typically offer lower risk to the firm, since it can use more of its existing strengths (improving prospects for success) while reducing transition costs by imposing generally lower stress on its existing resources and competences. The result can be to permit some of the portfolio benefits of diversifying away risk, while still capitalizing upon the strengths and capabilities which derive from specialization.

Further, it should be evident that the characteristics of markets in which the firm may choose to increase or decrease its investments will inevitably have some impact upon its performance. While all may be in a process of convergence to general equilibrium, at any one point some markets are more competitive, while others may afford better margins due to a variety of factors including market imperfections, government regulations and so on. Thus, as we earlier argued (Chapter 3), one of the major responsiblities of the marketing department is to identify and to recommend to senior management the markets in which the firm should be operating. In this respect, the corporate role of marketing is very clear. What is less clear, however, is by what process, using which criteria, should top management choose among these alternatives?

CHANGING CRITERIA FOR INVESTMENT DECISIONS

Traditionally, companies have approached their investment decisions from an accounting-driven perspective. For purposes of reporting upon the results of company operations, the accountants have developed an internally consistent and in many ways sophisticated set of interrelated concepts which enable the description of a complex set of economic activities in a commonly understood manner. This system, however, has contained within it the seeds of major problems with respect to the understanding of the true economics of business decisions. One of the areas which can pose difficulty lies in the area of what constitutes an investment. Accounting defines an investment as an expenditure made in one period, from which benefits are derived over several periods. In fact, the conventions of accounting typically depart from this basis, often aided and abetted by government taxation accounting policies. Thus, the purchase of land, buildings or equipment are commonly viewed and treated as investments—as assets—by businessmen and their accountants alike. The truth is, however, that they are not assets at all unless they are useful in helping create a profit—i.e., unless they serve viable markets.

Whether the accounting definitions have driven the phenomenon, or whether it results from the economies of relative scarcity in earlier eras, the fact remains that investment decisions have more typically been recognized as those revolving around such issues as which products, technologies or facilities rather than which customers, markets or applications. The arbitrariness of investment/expense distinctions is of course recognized in a modern discounted cash flow (d.c.f.) approach to analyzing investment decisions, in which it matters not one whit whether money is spent on advertising or furniture. Yet, as the cash flow mentality has taken root and the tools of d.c.f. analysis disseminated, a further shift has taken place. It is almost as though the result of taking the mystique out of the method has awakened recognition of the basic problem—namely: no matter how refined the methods of investment analysis, the results of such an analysis are no better than the information which is fed in. In other words, investment analysis can be described by the same acronym used to describe the computer's shortcomings: GIGO—Garbage In, Garbage Out.

Naturally, the problems of accurately estimating the future prices, volumes, and costs necessary to perform a discounted cash flow analysis are in some cases relatively straightforward. Thus, for incremental investments in growth options involving existing products and existing markets, better accuracies and lower variances might be expanded. However, for major strategic moves across existing product/market boundaries, for example, the uncertainties are much greater, and the accuracy of the estimates much reduced. Further, without passing judgment about motive, it is also very clear that knowledge of company hurdle rates[4] is quite easily gained—by inference or otherwise—such that forecast returns become subject to the danger of manipulation. As one controller put it to me:

> . . . I had never in my life seen investment proposal promising a 45% d.c.f. until I raised our hurdle rate about six months ago. Since then I've seen three of them!

Thus, financial practitioners, more than any other group, are typically well aware of the problems associated with the traditional and even the newer ways of evaluating investment decisions. They have typically learned to look cynically upon the estimates provided for them, tending to view many sales and marketing managers as pie-in-the-sky optimists, often reducing expenditure and revenue forecasts contained in investment proposals in a (sometimes misplaced) quest for more conservative, less risky scenarios. Naturally, such approaches can lead to ill will and internecine conflict, for if not well managed, the whole nature of the traditional process is to produce polarization between proponents of a proposal and those who judge it, who are too easily seen as its opponents.

There are, however, other approaches. One way, of course, is to attempt to deal with risk explicitly — *via* sensitivity analysis or even full-blown simulation, for example. This approach is less embraced than might be imagined,[5] although there is no doubt informal evaluation and analysis of this type. The *de facto* response of choice to the problem has been different. It has been to move away from a focus on the numbers themselves, toward a focus on the assumptions which underlie them. In the process, firms have typically moved from an inwardly-oriented perspective on their investment decisions, to one which is much more outwardly oriented. Instead of accepting *per se* management's sales growth forecasts, companies are more likely to ask what is the future growth rate of the market in which the product will be sold. Instead of questioning forecast product sales volumes, there is more attention focused on market share, either now or in the future. Going further, some may ask against which companies the firm will be competing, what is the likely future market structure, how will technology in this business be changing, and other such questions. The key point is not that these questions can usually be answered with any great precision, but that in the process of asking and attempting to answer such questions the company's management is *explicitly* addressing the issue of the validity of the assumptions which underlie the financial projections.

The answers to such questions are typically sought and assessed within the framework of strategic portfolio analysis. Such approaches have been at the core of many companies' shifts in planning orientation which have taken place since the mid-Seventies. They are probably best viewed not as an alternative way of setting investment priorities, but rather as an additional way of doing so. They provide a systematic, organized and relatively easily communicated way of assembling, assessing and integrating a variety of information helpful in setting investment priorities and thus setting strategic directions. They have been instrumental in bringing about a shift of focus in many companies, as summarized in Table 4-1. The right way to interpret Table 4-1 is, however, in complementary fashion. Clearly it was quite wrong to have emphasized solely the financial aspects of investment decisions with so little regard for strategic considerations. However, it would be quite irresponsible to advocate a focus on strategic factors without also considering their financial implications. As we noted earlier, it is the firm's financial officers who have been faced with the enormous problems which have sometimes resulted from the traditional approach. Far from being opposed to these newer ideas, many are only too eager to find thoughtul approaches that can help improve the quality of the key investment decisions of the firm. It is these approaches that we will now consider directly.

TABLE 4-1   Investment Decisions and Strategic Direction

	TRADITIONAL	NEW
Investment Decision Focus	Product/Technologies/ Facilities	Markets/Customers/ Applications
General Approach	Financially and Budgetarily Oriented	Market and Competitively Oriented
Key Concerns	Derived Profit and Cash Flow Numbers	Analysis of Basic Market and Competitive Factors Underlying the Numbers
Typical Measures	ROI→DCF/Present Value/IRR	Market Size, Market Growth, Competitive Strengths, Market Potentials, etc.
Tools	Capital Budgeting	Strategic Portfolio Analysis

PORTFOLIO APPROACHES TO SETTING STRATEGIC DIRECTION

A substantial number of approaches to portfolio analysis have been developed over the last ten to fifteen years. It is fair to say, however, that in general we have witnessed a movement which began with more straightforward and simple schema and progressed toward increasingly complex systems. Accordingly, we have organized this section of the chapter in similar manner, beginning with a review of the Boston Consulting Group's four-box matrix based upon the two variables of market share and market (segment) growth, and proceeding to the more elaborate schemes which were subsequently developed.

The Growth Share Matrix

The matrix of the Boston Consulting Group (BCG) is based upon two key dimensions of growth of market or market segment in which the product or business competes and market-share position relative to competitors. The matrix is constructed by cross-arraying these dimensions to create a fourfold classification system, as shown in Table 4-2.

TABLE 4-2   The Growth Share Matrix

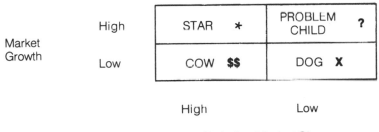

		High	Low
Market Growth	High	STAR *	PROBLEM CHILD ?
	Low	COW $$	DOG X

High   Low

Relative Market Share

Rather than showing absolute market share, we compute relative market share, which is equal to your market share divided by the market share of your largest competitor. This measure has the attractive property of indicating when you become the dominant (largest) competitor in a particular market or segment, for then relative market share is greater than 1.0. A further advantage of computing relative market share is that it removes the effects of market structure. Typically, an absolute market share of, say, 40% means something different in a two- or three-competitor market from what it means in a ten-competitor market. When reviewing an overall corporate or divisional portfolio, a variety of market structures may be represented, rendering a display using absolute market share ambiguous in terms of the company's competitive position in its various product-markets.

On the vertical axis, since we wish to use the matrix to help us set future strategic direction and thereby guide our investment strategy, we should be focusing on future (forecast) market growths. Since we are dealing with strategic issues, we should be considering long-term or trend growth rate, not short term, and for most industries a three- to five-year horizon is appropriate. In terms of market measures, there is a general tendency to use measures of physical units of some form (pounds, meters, tons, units, etc.) which most of the time are adequate. It is worth noting, however, that under conditions of severe price competition unit growth may even be associated with shrinking dollar prices, and in these situations, in particular, dollar (revenue) measures (towards which this author is in any case biased) must be weighted much more heavily — for, after all, profit (expressed in currency units) is the end game.

In application, considerable controversy usually arises over where to place the cut point that divides "high growth" from "low growth" markets. Obviously there can be no absolute standard, but many companies have found it helpful to develop a rule relating the cut point to an underlying measure of overall economic growth, such as G.N.P. or G.D.P. Clearly, managers of businesses or products competing in slower growth markets will typically seek a lower cutoff and *vice versa*. Wherever the level is set, the key point is to ensure some external criterion and *not* to base the decision on an internal criterion (such as average corporate growth rate) which may be biased by poor corporate performance. In a typical portfolio businesses will be distributed along the vertical axis in any case, so that much of the agonizing over choice of cut point is misplaced and akin to the internal transfer pricing debates which sometimes divert management's attention from the true challenges facing the firm, which are usually external in origin.

In BCG's approach to portfolio analysis, there is a strong emphasis on the correlation which often exists between the financial characteristics of a product and its market position and direction. For example, businesses and products with high shares of the market they are serving are typically more profitable. Similarly, businesses which are increasing their volume quickly (growing market share) may develop voracious appetites for cash. In general, these correlations are supported by empirical research such as that of PIMS,[6] and may also be derived from the experience curve arguments of BCG.

The fourfold typology therefore results in four types of businesses, often given the names indicated in Table 2. Many companies and managers find these names a hindrance rather than a help, and other naming schemes are often resorted to — particularly for "dog" businesses. We shall use the neutral descriptive form for the section headlines which follow. These sections briefly outline the predicted financial characteristics of the four types of business, and then discuss alternative objectives and broad strategies.

High Growth Market/Low Market Share

Often known as problem children, lottery tickets or wildcats, this category of products is generally thought of as a very risky investment. Growth markets often exhibit a great deal of uncertainty. Technology of product and process are still often evolving while customer usage patterns and purchase frequencies, as well as ultimate market potential, may still be indeterminate. From a financial perspective, this business is often marginally profitable and, while growing its volume, will consume a considerable amount of cash for increased fixed investment and working capital. If sufficient cash is not provided, the market share of the product relative to competition cannot improve, and the result will eventually be a slide downward to the bottom right-hand quadrant.

From a strategic perspective, this is often viewed as a double-or-quit business. In other words, at first sight it would appear that the company faces a clear-cut choice — either build share and target the product for market dominance or exit the business by either gradual or more immediate means. In fact, of course, other options are available. Indeed, since only one company can become dominant in a particular market, only one competitor can win this game, so that any others who seek dominance are bound to lose. The other options all focus around strategies of segmentation, whereby the company attempts to find a niche in the marketplace. Such a niche is of little use if it provides only temporary refuge — i.e. the company must be able to defend its niche and maintain dominance over it for this to be an effective strategy. The attractiveness of such options are clear, however, for whereas the double-or-quit approach produces only a single winner scenario, segmentation strategies involving niche selection and dominance can produce multiple-win scenarios. In other words, under this option multiple competitors can each dominate segments of the market and coexist reasonably harmoniously. Henderson has pointed out that such coexistence rests upon sound ecological as well as economic principles.[7]

High Growth Market/High Market Share

These star businesses are much beloved yet relatively rare. As a star becomes more dominant in its market and market growth begins to slow, not only does this business look more and more profitable, its cash flows will also begin to improve. Very asset-intensive businesses will, of course, be heavy cash consumers while growing, but for many others the cash flow picture is less acute.

In terms of business objectives and strategies, the generally accepted recommendation is to ensure a dominant market position such that as market growth slows, the product will end up securing the cash cow title, thereby becoming an important source of funds to support future growth businesses. A frequent danger is that management is tempted to manage for profit too early, thus compromising market position to the point where ultimate achievement of the cash cow position will be lost to a competitor. The converse problem may also occur, particularly with the type of aggressive growth-hungry management which often gravitates to this type of business or product. Thus, at some point, the decision to stop gaining share must be taken and acted upon. A variety of factors may affect the timing of this decision, but such influences as the firm's alternative investment opportunities, market structure (number of competitors), buyer preferences (e.g., desire for second or third source, etc.) and so on will usually have some impact. Often, however, operating management will find it difficult to reverse the momentum of the business so that volume and share gain may continue for too long. If decisions to hold share and maximize current returns are taken earlier in the cycle, there will be a corresponding need for a high degree of innovation to sustain growth (and profits) over the longer term.

In segmented markets, it is entirely possible for the stars to be white dwarfs — i.e., competitors may dominate their segments but the market may be so fragmented that returns are in no case particularly large. These same segments as they emerge, however, may be a source of great danger to the market leader, for he neglects them at the peril of his overall leadership. It is obviously not necessary to compete in all segments, but new segments that will grow to substantial size must be entered if leadership is to be maintained. The history of markets is full of leaders' late responses to such changes leading ultimately to loss of leadership. Similar threats can be posed by technological change.

Low Growth Market/High Market Share

Continuing our progression around the matrix, we arrive next at the cash cow. Since at this point the market is growing slowly, if at all, and we have already achieved dominant share position, reinvestment needs drop sharply and cash flow grows correspondingly. If well managed, the cost position of this product should be superior to that of its competitors, and it should be highly profitable.

This category takes its common name (Table 4-2) from what should be the primary objective in managing this kind of business: cash flow. In many cases this will translate into strategy of holding share, for the maturity stage of low or zero growth frequently can last quite a long time. Availability of better investment alternatives and threats to the existing business such as regulation or radically new technology may lead to a decision to fully or partially liquidate market position. Thus, instead of milking the cow for cash, management initiates a deliberate harvesting strategy aimed at increasing short term cash flows, at the expense of market position. Strategies which may facilitate achieving such enhanced cash-flow objectives include increasing price, reducing or even eliminating certain kinds of service, retracting distribution, etc.

It is perhaps unfortunate that managers zealous for short-term earnings and cash have frequently sought to over-milk cash cows. While it is certainly possible to over-invest in mature products and businesses, so is it also easy to under-invest and over-milk.[8] Without the willingness to reinvest, costs may become uncompetitive and competitive position will deteriorate. The experience of the United States' auto and steel industries illustrates clearly the dangers of failure to reinvest in maturing businesses, and the pressures imposed on cash flows during good years by shareholders, unions, management and even government can sometime combine to severely harm long-term position.

The other difficulty which often occurs with cash cows is that even when the primary objective is defined as cash flow, and the volume goal as share maintenance, operating management will continue to pursue volume and share growth. As the overall market matures, however, it often becomes relatively inelastic. Diminishing returns will then set in, while the level of competitive spending is needlessly and unprofitably escalated. The consequences are to inhibit cash-generating capability and render returns less than satisfactory. The situation in such oligopolistic competition may be compared to that of the nuclear arms race, where the balance of weaponry terror continues to rise to the true benefit of none but the armaments producers (e.g. advertising agency).

In summary then, the cash cow is supposed to be the primary source of cash in the portfolio, and the bulk of that cash will be funneled to support growth elsewhere, in newer markets and/or products. Dangers of both over- and under-investing in cows are rife, and demand a skilled balancing act from senior managers.

Low Growth Market/Low Market Share

The somewhat pejoratively named dogs are in fact the commonest type of the four. They are, if you like, the backbone of industry, for since only a minority of markets are fast growing, and in any one market only one com petitor can be dominant, it follows that the majority of products and businesses end up in the bottom right-hand corner.

From a financial perspective, the relative cost position of the dog is now crucial. If management has kept costs competitive, and if management of the industry leader has been dilatory (as often occurs), then dogs of reasonable scale can be quite productive. If, however, the cow has the superior cost position — as BCG would argue should be the case if they have done their job properly — then the financial position of all but the strongest of dogs will be very weak, and may easily be rendered untenable by some aggression on the part of the market leader.

In general, then, dogs will be managed with the idea of trying to maximize cash flow, but it should be evident that the tenor of competition in their market will have a major impact on their financial profile. Thus, the cash generation goal is frequently stymied by competitive conditions. Further, the attitude of many managements is to persist in attempting to increase the volume and share of these products, which usually worsens industry competitive conditions substantially, as well as deteriorating the cash position of the product yet further.

Despite the doom which often surrounds being designated as a dog, however, they offer a multitude of interesting strategic options. Yet, since many of these options involve some substantial restructuring of the businesses, they are frequently deferred by management, which seems to prefer incremental attempts to turn around the business. The well-known aversion to write-offs of many professional managers may be a factor in delaying restructuring, but that many eventually despair of such efforts is, no doubt, partially responsible for the very large number of divestitures in the United States during the 1975-80 period.

The key to managing dogs to any salvation other than liquidation or other forms of exit is to focus strenuously on cash flow. Accounting profit and projected profitabilities mean little for these competitively vulnerable businesses which may conceivably have few years of life ahead of them anyway. One of the classic dog strategies, however, is resegmentation of some type. In other words, just as we might have sought to reposition a problem child toward dominance in a niche, so we might seek to do so with a dog. The trick now is to do it without significant outflows of cash! In some cases this may not be difficult, particularly if management is willing to accept the notion that it might be better to be smaller, profitable and cash-positive than larger, unprofitable and cash-negative. In the United States, at least, this philosophy makes good sense to owners, owner-managers and shareholders, although it is sometimes resisted by the professional manager. Yet it should be evident that making a business smaller *per se* will rarely improve its financial position and in some cases may even cause deterioration of the operating economics. Resegmentation must, if it is to succeed, enable the firm to achieve good operating economics while deterring entry into the niche by competition. One way in which this might be achieved is geographic resegmentation. In any distribution-cost-intensive business this can produce important cash flow benefits, and there has been widespread use of this strategy by the oil companies to improve cash flows from their filling station operations. Similar resegmentation has been practiced by railway systems and airlines. Other ways to resegment which may be successful include greater specialization, which has worked quite well for some specialty car makers like Mercedes and BMW, but can sometimes prove disastrous if strong and determined competitors enter the niche, a not unlikely phenomenon if margins are high and growth difficult to find elsewhere. Sustaining a specialized niche in a maturing market is therefore often difficult, unless that niche can be found in a segment which is growing or can be made to grow. Although this sounds impossible, such opportunities exist in many markets, and Miller's United States' success with their light beer, "Lite", BMW's surge in the sports sedan segment of the automobile market and Sony's brilliant Walkman all illustrate the possibilities.

Similar opportunities may arise from a new technology or new approach to an existing market. Nucor's profitable performance in the U.S. steel industry during the 1970's was based on its commitment to electric arc furnace mini-mill steel technology, while the more recent growth of airlines like People Express or Rent-a-Wreck (used car rental) have been based on such different approaches.

More adventurous strategies for dogs will often devolve from analysis of industry structure. It is quite common to find that returns for all producers are low in mature markets, one of the major reasons being excess capacity optimistically installed during the heady days of market growth. The strategists' primary focus must then be upon rationalization of capacity — for as long as there is significant overhang, price competition is likely to be severe and debilitating. Often one or two competitors will begin to pursue a so-called kennel of dogs strategy of merging and absorbing minor competitors while reducing industry total capacity. Such a strategy has been successfully pursued in the United States white goods (major appliance) industry by White Consolidated Industries, although other mergers of dogs, such as British Leyland and Citroen-Peugeot have had more starred existences. Interestingly, kenneling is rarely pursued by the dominant competitor (cash cow) but does offer a possibly less cash-intensive means to compete with him for the number two, three or four company in the industry.

In other cases, steps short of full acquisition or merger may help the dog. Joint production or component coproduction can reduce capital requirements and the dangers of excess capacity, as well as hedging balance sheet risks. In maturing industries with escalating capital and innovation costs, such strategies are now widespread and the worldwide car industry offers many examples — *viz.* Nissan/VW, Nissan/Alfa Romeo, Honda/British Leyland, Volvo/Renault/Citroen-Peugeot (V6 Engines), Chrysler/Mitsubishi, Ford/Toyo Kogyo, Isuzu/G.M., Toyota/G.M. and Suzuki/G.M. (the last two mooted at time of writing).

Other options for dogs, short of liquidation, prove most difficult to pursue profitably. The desirability of reducing vertical integration and becoming more flexible, more "assembly-oriented," are suggested by the basic strategic view that one of the major advantages of small companies is their ability to move quickly, and by the empirical studies of the PIMS program.[9] However, such strategic moves are usually based on a market strategy of finding new niches quicker, exploiting them and moving on. If the niches become significant, they are liable to invasion by competitors, to the detriment of the dog. American Motors in the United States has had a history of finding niches and losing them to other competitors. In the 1970's, for example, their successful exploitation of four wheel drive attracted first Subaru and more recently Toyota (with the Tercel station wagon) and their share dropped badly.

A final dog option which could, we believe, be more usefully exploited by larger companies is a partial rather than full sell-down. In some cases the true economics of dogs are worsened by the corporate overhead charges they carry. A reduced equity position, with more operating autonomy for management could certainly improve the economic results of many dogs although this approach obviously has some other dangers.

Growth-Share Matrices: An Evaluation

It has become fashionable to debunk the BCG contribution in some quarters, but for the most part the criticism is ill-founded, and is a consequence of the naive and even foolish ways in which the concept has been employed by some managers. It has been said that a little knowledge is dangerous, and that is certainly the case here. The appeal of the growth-share matrix lies in its overwhelming simplicity and its attractive depiction of important aspects of products' strategic positions. Yet it should be evident to all but the most unthinking of observers that the world of oligopolistic competition is not simple — it is in fact complex and subtle. The straightforward application of any decision rule in such an environment is likely to redound upon the perpetrator if only because rendering oneself too predictable can be disastrous.

The growth-share matrix should be viewed as a way of helping clarify thinking about the strategic objectives we should be pursuing for particular businesses, and as a means of suggesting some alternative strategic options. It should not be applied with great rigidity, and viewed as a way of prescribing strategies. Used in this way, it can be positively dangerous. For example, consider four competitors in a high-growth market, with one clearly dominant. The three with problem children, if they act naively, could simultaneously conclude they should seek dominant share — which could have calamitous consequences for all four producers.

In fact, it can be argued that one of the major weaknesses of the growth-share matrix is the tendency of its first-order prescriptions to promote competitive *convergence*. Much more desirable would be an approach which promoted at least some degree of competitive *divergence* — the principle of "to each his own." Further, we might cite some additional limitations of the matrix. For example, market share and market growth are in most views important strategic variables. Yet there are a variety of other important factors — PIMS would suggest at least thirty-seven — which should also be considered. Supply vulnerability has been a major concern for Japan, and became so for many U.S. companies during the 1970's. Thus, as a number of the international oil companies found out, market share doesn't mean very much without crude oil! Further, all is not delight in growth markets, and a number of companies, including Smorgon Consolidated Industries of Australia, seem to find particular joy in entering relatively mature markets. In addition, PIMS research suggests the importance of asset intensity in understanding the economics and competitive conditions of an industry. Certainly, BCG's cash flow arguments are much more visible and compelling in heavily asset-intensive industries.

As a result of these concerns, many companies have moved to extend and modify the basic concept of portfolio analysis by developing more inclusive systems which are often labeled policy matrices. We shall be examining a couple of these fairly briefly in the remaining section of the chapter. It is worth pointing out, however, that it is possible to view all of these systems (including BCG's matrix) as a way of formalizing some basic concepts which have been long established in business policy. Thus, the BCG approach can be viewed as a special case of a more general framework.

The general framework embraces the idea that there are really two components involved in assessing alternatives. The first is the attractiveness of the investment opportunity. High growth markets are generally viewed as more attractive than low or negative growth markets. However, as we earlier noted, other factors may also have an influence on attractiveness — such aspects as susceptibility to regulation, environmental hazard and security of supply might be examples. As we noted, then, BCG's choice of market growth may be viewed as one way to measure attractiveness.

Unfortunately, an attractive market opportunity does not profit guarantee. The second key idea involves whether or not we can win the competitive battle to capitalize on that opportunity — our relative strength. Thus, market opportunities tend to attract a variety of competitors — yet for us to prosper our firm must be able to achieve a full or partial win over competition. Competitors often screen on similar criteria to ourselves (particularly if we all use market growth!), so that many apparently "attractive" markets are characterized by high numbers of failed competitors, drawn like moths to the light. Hence the second key factor which we must assess is our chance of winning over competitors. Traditional business policy approaches would argue that our prospects of succeeding are best if our competitive strengths match the requirements of a particular opportunity — an approach which is also consistent with the policy matrix notion. We now examine two policy matrices, as examples of the way in which companies have developed the concept.

The General Electric Business Screen

Initially developed in the late 1960's, working together with the management consultant McKinsey, the General Electric Business Screen (variously known as the stoplight system, the ninebox and even simply as the grid) is one of the better known, extended policy matrices. In these systems the two axes are described as market attractiveness and business position. Each business is assessed with respect to the strength of its position, and the attractiveness of its market. The individual businesses are then depicted in a two-dimensional display, as shown in Table 4-3.

Each of the axes is, of course, a summary or composite measure. Some of the measures which might be considered in assessing market attractive-

TABLE 4-3   General Electric—Type Policy Matrix

		Strong	Medium	Weak
MARKET ATTRACTIVENESS	High	Green	Green	Amber
	Medium	Green	Amber	Red
	Low	Amber	Red	Red

STRENGTH OF BUSINESS POSITION

ness and strength of position are shown in Table 4-4. Such a listing is typically developed from a review of those which other companies have used, empirical research such as that of the PIMS program or in-company proprietary studies, and the prior experience of the company and its executives. At General Electric, the measures have evolved over the years, and fewer are used now than previously.[10] The development of the measures and the weights applied to each, the methods by which different opportunities are identified and assessed, and the management process involved in implementing this type of policy matrix are all important issues which must be addressed.[11]

The net result of the analysis, however, is to place each of the businesses or products being analyzed into a position on the matrix (shown in Table 4-3). The resulting position will suggest a general direction for the investment strategy with respect to each opportunity. General Electric uses different colors to signify this direction, hence the "stoplight" name. "Green" businesses will generally be candidates for investment and growth. "Red" for milking, harvesting and divesting, while the "Amber" businesses are frequently the most difficult to decide upon, often requiring a very selective approach to investment and strategy development (see Table 4-3).

TABLE 4-4 Sample Underlying Measures for Assessing Market Attractiveness and Strength of Business Position

Strength of Business Position	Market Attractiveness
Market Share	Market Size
Profitability Record	Market Potential
Liquidity	Market Growth
Financial Leverage	Market Segments
Operating Leverage	Key Competitors
Capacity	Technological Change
Technological Expertise	Barriers to Entry
Modernity of Plant and Equipment	Barriers to Exit
Raw Materials Position	Regulatory Constraints
Union Relations	Social Factors
Government Relations	Union Representation
Management Capabilities	Degree of Vertical Integration

The policy matrix approach can be used in an auditing context to assess current position, as well as projectively to develop momentum forecasts of current strategy and identify future strategic options. As with the growth-share matrix, however it is important to bear in mind that this type of policy matrix is to be used as an aid to strategy development — not a substitute for it!

Arthur D. Little Maturity/Competitive Position Matrix

As if wanting to go more than one better, the A.D. Little System generates a total of twenty cells in the matrix shown below.

TABLE 4-5   A.D. LITTLE POLICY MATRIX

Stage of Industry Maturity

Competitive Position	Embryonic	Growth	Mature	Aging
Dominant				
Strong				
Favorable				
Tenable				
Weak				

The industry maturity concept is drawn straight from the idea of the market life cycle so familiar to marketing managers. Little suggests seven factors which help in assessing industry maturity. These include not only market growth rate (a variable appearing in virtually all policy matrices) but such factors as industry potential, product line breadth, number of competitors, market share stability, purchasing patterns, ease of entry, and technology. These factors are used to help management assess where the industry being evaluated stands with respect to its stage of evolution.

Evaluating competitive strengths is a more elaborate process, and a list of thirty-seven criteria are used to help in this process. Although it would not be appropriate to discuss all of these, factors such as market share position, as might be expected, are important, but such additional criteria as capacity utilization, cost position, breadth of product line, price leadership, technological strength and so on are also included.

One of the rich aspects of the A.D. Little system is the multitude of strategic options enumerated for managers. These are developed for categories of market, product line, operations, managerial systems and so on. An accompanying problem might be the failure to integrate what are basically functional options into a unified thrust. Little avoids this, first by showing each of the enumerated options to have a natural period of the maturity cycle during which they are executed, then using this notion to introduce the idea of strategic thrusts consistent with the business position in the maturity/competitive position matrix. This performs the needed integrative role, while also explicitly listing strategy options for all but two of the twenty cells in Table 4-5. Thus, for a weak position in an aging market there is an unequivocal charge to withdraw, while retrenchment is viewed as the only option for a tenable position in such a market. As a general purpose system, the A.D. Little method offers a pretty comprehensive approach to setting priorities and the development of business strategies.

Multifactor Portfolio Systems: An Assessment

The last few years seem to have witnessed more companies adopting multifactor approaches to assessing their business investment opportunities. Typically an evolutionary path in the use of portfolio analysis is followed.[12] In many cases, companies have begun with the simple four-box and eventually developed more complex schemata to be used in parallel with or even to replace the growth-share matrix. In many cases this evolution has occurred for praiseworthy reasons, e.g. the concern to introduce more "realism" in the schemes leads often to the inclusion of more variables in a multifactor scheme. In some cases, however, the motives are more questionable. As we have seen, both the labels and the first-order strategy options of the four-box are rather uncompromising. Even though it is only one version of reality, that version is sufficiently threatening to some companies that, rather like an ostrich with its head in the sand, they change their portfolio system to avoid direct or threatening implications! The desire to avoid reality, while understandable, is scarcely a prescription for long life as a manager or as a company!

It is important to recognize, nonetheless, that the world is not composed of binary choices, nor described completely by market growth rates and market shares. More complex systems *can* be more realistic and richer in generating options. Further, the vaunted relationship between market characteristics and financial performance is, as we have noted, correlational and not directly causal. For example, there are many cash cows (measured by growth and share) that are not cash cows! Another school of thought might argue that the financial characteristics *per se* should be weighted more heavily than they are in a growth-share matrix.

Realism and complexity, however, bring problems in their train. The issues of which factors to include and how they should be weighted are often key bones of contention in more complex systems. The subjectivity of some of the factors leaves scope for honest men to disagree in their assessments, and in the "real world" there is a danger that organizational politics and power relationships may play an undue role. Some of these problems can be ameliorated by reference to such empirical results as the PIMS study in selecting and weighting factors, and by managing the process well. However, although both the simpler growth-share matrix and more complex policy matrices are both susceptible to this kind of manipulation, there is little doubt that the latter are more susceptible. Further, as a result of greater complexity and subjectivity, it is understandably more difficult to explain to others in the organization why a particular business or product ends up in a particular position. We have compared the characteristics of these two approaches in the table below:

TABLE 4-6   Comparison of Portfolio Approaches

Growth-Share Matrix	Extended Policy Matrices
Simple	More Complex
More Objective	More Subjective
Easy to Communicate	Complicated to Communicate
Sparse	Rich
Easy to Implement	More Difficult to Implement
Lacks Realism	May Be More Realistic
May Lead to Competitive Convergence	Tend to Produce Competitive Divergence

In reviewing the comparison above, it should be evident that the growth-share matrix has much to commend it. It would be churlish indeed to leave this subject without commending the Boston Consulting Group for their very real contribution to the art and science of strategy. In a recent Columbia University study of corporate planners of the Fortune "500", BCG concepts were rated the most influential outside source of ideas on strategy in the nineteen-seventies.[13] Quite simply, it is close to an ideal system for getting started in the portfolio analysis and strategic marketing planning. It focusses on important variables which should in any case be known, arrays them in a way which makes intuitive and empirical sense and is visually appealing, it focusses management's attention on important issues, and best of all, it is the easiest system to learn and implement — a key factor in assisting companies to make the transition to more strategic management.[14]

Down the road a little, augmentation and evolution is much more easily promoted, once the basic concept has been mastered and disseminated. It is here that the virtues of more complex schemes are more likely to be manifest. Without exposure to the basic discipline, however, the results are likely to be a dissipated wishy-washy evaluation system which has little or no influence on management's decisions.

SUMMARY AND CONCLUSIONS

In the chapter, we have reviewed the relationship of marketing to corporate strategy, focussing in particular on the key interfaces involved via the strategic planning process. We began by pointing out the vital importance of market choice to the firm's strategy and performance. Consistent with our description of the marketing or outward-oriented firm, it is important to recognize that the company invests in customers and markets as well as products and technologies. The product/market composition of the firm is an important concern of corporate strategy, and the role of marketing is a vital one in managing customer/market inputs to that top management decision. Among the tools used to facilitate that input, the most important developments of the last fifteen years or so have focussed around portfolio analysis. We reviewed the origins of the approach in BCG's growth/share matrix quite closely, pointing out that it is a thinking person's aid to objective and strategy development. It is dangerous if misused by unthinking managers as a *substitute* for strategy development. Some companies have evolved more comprehensive and extensive approaches to portfolio analysis, which we dubbed policy matrices. Such approaches can produce substantial additional insight, and provide valuable assistance to strategy development. As with the simpler system, however, much depends on how they are used. Portfolio analysis is a useful addition to management's weaponry for strategic battles. To expect magical solutions to complex business problems, however, is asking too much. We fully expect these approaches to be assimilated and to fall into place as part of the management process in well-managed companies. The test of time is more likely to put them into perspective than anything else.

REFERENCES AND FOOTNOTES

1. H. Igor Ansoff, *Corporate Strategy*, New York, N.Y., McGraw-Hill, 1965. p. 109.

2. John M. Brion, *Corporate Marketing Planning*, New York: John Wiley, 1967, pp. 155-156.

3. Richard P. Rumelt, *Strategy, Structure, and Economic Performance*, Cambridge, Mass.: Harvard University Press, 1974.

4. The cutoff rate of return, below which investment proposals will not be funded.

5. William K. Hall, "Why Risk Analysis Isn't Working," *Long Range Planning*, December, 1975, pp. 25-29.

6. The acronym stands for the Profit Impact of Marketing Strategy, a collaborative data base and research project. The findings of this project do suggest, however, that there are a greater variety of variables influencing a business' performance than those heavily emphasized in the BCG product portfolio. For more details of the PIMS project see S. Schoeffler, R. D. Buzzell and D. F. Heany, "Impact of Strategic Planning on Profit Performance," *Harvard Business Review*, March-April 1974, pp. 137-145.

7. Bruce D. Henderson, *Henderson on Corporate Strategy*, Cambridge, Mass.: Abt Books, 1979.

8. Raymond Vernon, "Gone Are the Cash Cows of Yesteryear," *Harvard Business Review*, vol. 58, November-December, 1980, pp. 150-155.

9. See footnote 6, this chapter.

10. Yoram Wind and Vijay Mahajan, "Designing Product and Business Portfolios," *Harvard Business Review* Vol. 59, January-February, 1981, pp. 155-165.

11. Derek F. Abell and John S. Hammond, *Strategic Market Planning*, Englewood Cliffs, NJ: Prentice-Hall, 1979.

12. Philippe Haspeslagh, "Portfolio Planning: Uses and Limits," *Harvard Business Review* January-February 1982, pp. 58-73.

13. Noel Capon, John U. Farley and James M. Hulbert, *Strategic Planning in United States Manufacturing Companies*, New York City: Columbia University, manuscript in preparation.

14. Frederick W. Gluck, Stephen P. Kaufman and A. Steven Walleck, "Strategic Management for Competitive Advantage," *Harvard Business Review*, July-August 1980, pp. 154-161.

5

DEVELOPING BUSINESS UNIT STRATEGIES

The previous chapter indicated that as corporations grow, they typically become more complex, as their mix of products and markets becomes almost inevitably more diverse. As we noted, the way in which this diversity is managed is key to achievement of long term corporate objectives. When faced with complex problems, the typical response of a decision maker is to attempt to factor that complex problem into a series of simpler subproblems.[1] Such has been the approach of corporations to the problems posed by their growth. The formation of product divisions and the ensuing organizational changes were early manifestations of this process among U.S. corporations,[2] but the 1970's witnessed a questioning of the adequacy of existing divisionalization as well as the form of decentralization which is often fostered.

In this chapter we first explore the new forms of organization which have been evolving around what are most commonly designated as "businesses" or "business units." After reviewing the bases for forming such units, we then introduce a framework for developing objectives and strategic options for such "businesses." The next section describes the basic options in more detail, and the chapter concludes with a summary.

DEFINING A BUSINESS

Whether a company defines its products and markets narrowly or broadly, eventually the growth opportunities lessen. The classic response to this state of affairs is to broaden the range of products offered. At some point, the product range becomes difficult to manage within one operating organization grouped around functions — a fact which may be more evident if the range were broadened by acquisition — and a reorganization eventually takes place, usually on the basis of forming product divisions. Divisionalization, then, may be seen as a means of dealing with increased complexity, pushing the level of business integration to a lower level in the organization. It is as important to notice, however, that the bases upon which divisions are formed are often quite varied, and, even if appropriate at one point, frequently become outdated by ongoing evolution of the corporation. Often, then, the divisional structure in a particular company may be a somewhat haphazard grouping together, usually based around products and technologies, which has resulted from an historical unfolding which includes acquisitions and divestitures, as well as internal development and shut-downs. As growth continues to increase the complexity of the corporation, the likelihood of anomalies which produce strategic conflict and operating the inefficiency also tends to increase, to the point where comprehensive re-thinking of organization structure becomes desirable.

Many United States' companies were going through this process in the late seventies. Indeed, in many cases regrouping and reorganization was undertaken as a prerequisite to or part of a process of instituting strategic planning. As these changes took place, however, the basis on which businesses were defined also evolved. There are basically five ways in which the mission of a business may be defined, in terms of resources, products or services, technologies, market or customer and function or need.[3] The latter two are demand (externally) driven, whereas the first three are more supply (internally) driven — or in other words, more consistent with the arguments expressed by Levitt in his classic "Marketing Myopia."[4] As Strategic Business Units (S.B.U.'s) have evolved from regrouping of divisions, the definition of mission has usually shifted, consistent with the change from internal to external orientation embraced by strategic planning, toward a more demand-driven perspective. The Strategic Planning Institute, for example, in advising members on how to prepare data for input to the PIMS program, urges them to define businesses based upon the extent to which products share common customers, competitors and costs. A.D. Little emphasizes these and other factors, including technology, distribution, geography and price structures of products.

In some companies, the shift to SBU's began by an attempt to better group activities together for planning purposes, and an operating structure later evolved from an informal or formal planning team. In any case, the net result has often been to increase lower level operating autonomy within an organized framework provided by a portfolio-based strategic planning system. Other benefits may include quicker response and more flexibility while encouraging a broader perspective on the corporation's activities by forcing integration on lower levels within the organization. When General Electric went through this process, for example, they ended up with forty-seven SBU's, each of which operated within the broad framework provided by GE's strategic planning system.

These entities, which are now commonly called businesses (but for which in some companies more conventional terminology like divisions or product groups may be more acceptable) have become the prime movers of strategy generation in many companies. It is at this level that the remainder of the chapter will focus.

ELEMENTS OF A BUSINESS UNIT STRATEGY

The major elements of a business unit strategy are discussed in this section. Although we deal with them sequentially, we also recognize that the process by which such strategies are developed is typically anything but sequential.

Determining the Strategic Direction and Options

The strategic direction of a business is typically not something which its managers decide upon alone. Whether the corporate guidance proffered results from a portfolio or policy matrix analysis, or comes from the more traditional approaches embraced by other managements, the corporate role in setting the direction is often marked and sometimes predominant. Nonetheless, there are basically only three options available in setting overall strategic direction, *viz.* to grow, to maintain, or to shrink a business. Regardless of position in a portfolio analysis these options are still open, although the weight of evidence would seem to support the idea that the prospects of successfully growing a business are greater in growth markets than in declining ones, and that "shrink" options are more likely to be used in the latter kind of market than the former.

Table 5-1 develops the elements of the strategy further. Notice that under each of the basic strategic directions outlined are some further options. In growing a business, for example, emphasis can be placed upon increasing the growth of existing business versus developing new business. The new SBU positioned in growing, elastic markets is likely to find the first emphasis provides more than ample opportunity to achieve its growth objectives. Over time, however, it usually evolves toward much heavier emphasis on the development of new business opportunities, whether focussed on new markets or new products.

Similar but perhaps more difficult choices arise under the "maintain" alternative. The central question is what shall be maintained — volume or profit? In the short run theere is always a very definite tradeoff between these two objectives. Furthermore, in slow-growing markets, the choice of which to emphasize becomes particularly acute. Whereas newer markets are likely to yield volume increases from either price decreases or cost-incurring improvements in quality, service, etc., this is less likely to occur in more mature markets, in which potential has been more fully exploited. As a result, strategies adopted in order to maintain volume may well lead to loss of margin and profit. It is for these reasons that a number of the portfolio approaches discussed in the previous chapter urge decreased emphasis on volume *per se* in more mature markets.

The shrink option is most likely to be pursued when the market is either in decline or is forecast to commence declining. Early warning of such decline is likely to lead to decisions to "harvest" the business over its remaining life. Lacking such warning, rather painful and immediate decision must typically be made, and it is difficult to avoid severe consequences for the bottom line, employees, suppliers and customers and the local and broader community. Normally, harvest options are relatively plentiful, and will include such possibilities as raising price, cutting service or breadth of distribution, eliminating or reducing promotional communications and the like.

Setting the strategic direction is a key issue for any business. As we noted earlier, the basic direction which is established may result from a portfolio analysis or some other approach. However, it is best defined, we believe, in a collaborative way, involving careful appraisal from a "top-down" perspective of where this business fits into the company's overall opportunity set, synthesized with the "bottom-up" knowledge of the prospects for this business which can come only from those intimately involved in its running. If matters come to a head, clearly "top-down" views will prevail, but to impose them without careful consideration of other views invites suboptimization. Perhaps the traditions of the Japanese "ringi" approach to decision making have much from which other cultures can learn, for lack of participaton in these kinds of key decisions can have disastrous consequences.

In summary, then, we should note that setting strategic direction is an essential prerequisite for strategy development. As the old saying goes, when you don't know where you want to go, any road will get you there. Helping to determine the basic direction to pursue with a business is the central concern of all portfolio and policy analyses systems. In the past, unfortunately, the importance of direction-setting was not always recognized. In many companies, the directions developed depended more upon the drive and political skill of division management than any other factor. In others, direction emerged by default, in a process the British call "muddling through" but which some American authors have taken to calling incrementalism.[5] In companies which are mastering the strategic planning process, however, direction is now clearly and unequivocally established. The change is, of course, not without its problems. It is fascinating to observe how middle managers who previously complained about lack of clear direction and objectives respond when the situation is remedied. Some would clearly prefer ambiguity to a clear direction with which they disagree and/or believe will be difficult to implement or achieve! Overall, however, better definition of strategic direction, accompanied usually by much greater differentiation of direction for different business units, are major outcomes that typically result from a shift to strategic planning.

Key Strategic Decisions

The options we have just described, and summarized in Figure 5-1, provide the framework around which the rest of the chapter is organized. However, in fleshing out these options, there are a number of key parameters — which we call key strategic decisions — which have to be dealt with in each case. These we will now explain.

Product/Market Mix Strategy is the first key area, and is one of the primary bases along which competitors' strategies are differentiated. Some businesses compete with a broad range of products, others specialize; some compete across the board in multiple markets and segments while others focus attention very narrowly, becoming segment or end-use specialists. Very often, product/market specialization covary. Thus, if we array alternatives as in Table 5-1, we note that four options emerge. The high-high combination we call the dominator mix and is the product/market posture often assumed by large companies; for example, General Motors in the car business. The low-low combination is the nicher, the frequent choice of smaller firms, whose businesses may even focus on single segments, sometimes with very limited product lines. Porsche and Morgan provide good examples in the car business. The low product mix, high market mix combination is the product specialist, making a limited line of product, but selling to a wide variety of markets. For obvious reasons, this option is a frequent choice of manufacturers, and because of investment limitations is frequently favored by manufacturers early in their existence. In the car industry, Honda's early strategy was a good example, as was that of Apple in the microcomputer business. The remaining option is that of market specialist. Because of the converse investment imperatives, this choice is much more commonly exercised by retail and distribution businesses than by manufacturers, but analogies can be found in earlier days of the car industry, before capital barriers became so high. A number of high quality European car producers, for example, focussed almost exclusively upon the sports-car segment, yet offered a wide variety of products to

FIGURE 5-1 Developing Business Unit Strategy

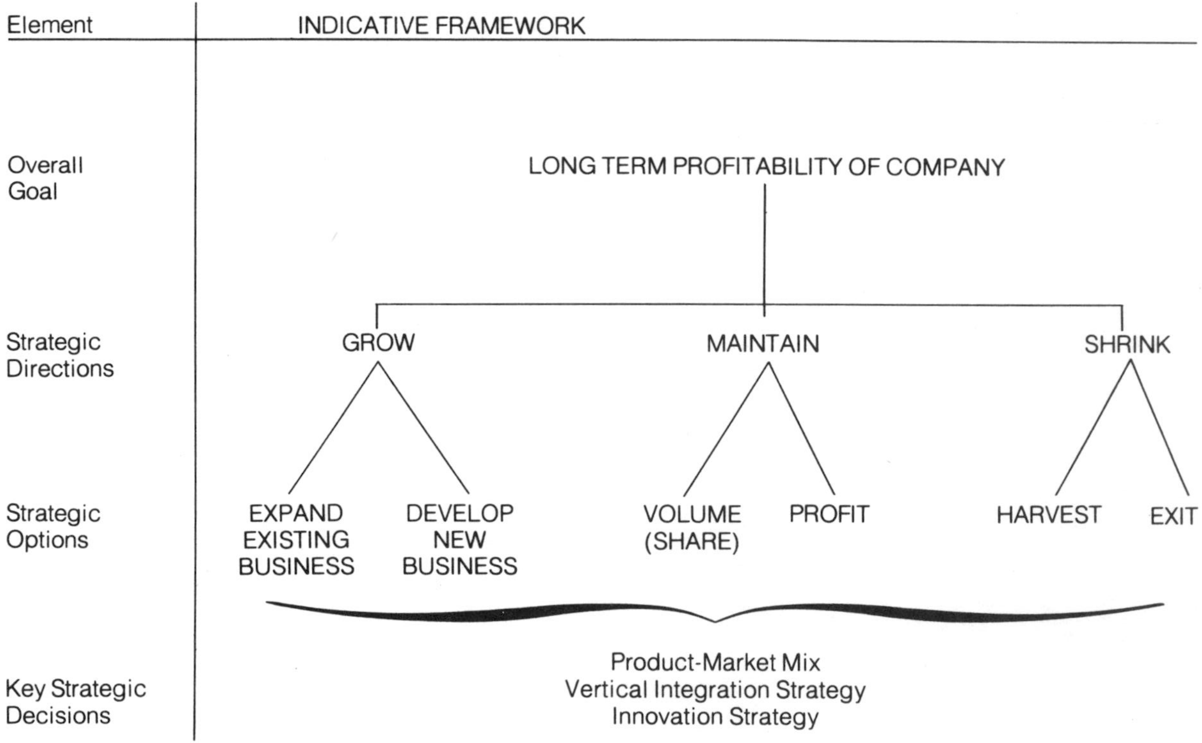

Element	INDICATIVE FRAMEWORK		
Overall Goal	LONG TERM PROFITABILITY OF COMPANY		
Strategic Directions	GROW	MAINTAIN	SHRINK
Strategic Options	EXPAND EXISTING BUSINESS / DEVELOP NEW BUSINESS	VOLUME (SHARE) / PROFIT	HARVEST / EXIT
Key Strategic Decisions	Product-Market Mix / Vertical Integration Strategy / Innovation Strategy		

those markets. Most noteworthy among these were the creations of Ettore Bugatti. Worth remembering, however, is the fact that even in the twenties and thirties when labor costs and capital requirements were lower, broad lines and narrow markets did not make for great profits. Bugatti is a name remembered today mainly by enthusiasts!

TABLE 5-1 Product Market Mix Strategy

Product Mix

		High	Low
Market Segment Mix	High	Dominator	Product Specialist
	Low	Market Specialist	Nicher

Obviously, the product/market mix strategy of the business is critically dependent upon the way the business (mission) is defined. Generally, market or function-based businesses need to beware of the danger of over-expanding product ranges, whereas product/technology/resource-based businesses are more likely to proliferate markets, and to be caught napping by indirect competitors who use different products/technologies/resources to meet the same need. Finally, it should also be recognized that the product/market mix strategy will — and typically must — evolve over time. If the business is operating in a very new market, product/market mix is usually low in variety. Very new markets are typically relatively undifferentiated with respect to customers and users, simply because they have not yet learned how the product can best meet their needs. Once they do so, however, they become more articulate in their choices, and the market will usually segment around these needs. Such has been the history of many markets — for example, the automobile, camera, calculator and copier markets. As a result, product heterogeneity will initially be low, and broaden as the market grows. Even if the business is entering the market at a later stage of development, however, product mix is usually limited initially by economic considerations (investment needs) as well as market uncertainty; the range will typically expand later. As the market and/or the business mature, however, product/market mix will inevitably begin to contract, diminishing of course to zero at exit. This expansion and contraction process will be explored in more depth later in the chapter as we discuss strategy options.

Vertical Integration Strategy is a second area where key decisions must be made. Although choice of strategy is in some countries legally constrained, particularly with respect to distribution arrangements, there remains considerable scope for discretion. Typically, businesses will be increasing their integration during the later growth phase of the market. During the introductory and early growth phase there is often too much market uncertainty for management to feel comfortable with further major commitments of assets, especially because their attention and efforts are rightfully often consumed by the fast growth taking place in the market. Later, when the market is mature, and decline may be in prospect, moves to reduce integration are more likely to improve performance.

Innovation Strategy is the final key decision area we shall review. Again, policy here should be carefully related to the maturity of market and the business unit itself. To enter markets in their very early development will demand a fairly strenuous effort in research and development relative to the business' competitors. On the other hand, as the market evolves to maturity and decline, the relative scale of effort is likely to change considerably. The PIMS study, for example, reports its members' businesses spent 10% of sales on Research and Development (R&D) in the start-up phase, 3% in the growth phase, 2% in the early maturity phase, and only 1% in late maturity. The focus will also change; as the evolving competitive pressures turn management's attention toward their relative cost position, so will the direction of R&D policy shift toward improving the economics of the business.

There are other basic issues with respect to innovation policy. With the exception of the very early stage of market development, where, by definition, only innovative companies can tread, management is faced with the basic choice of whether the business will attempt to compete by bringing some degree of innovation to the marketplace, or whether it will operate with a basically imitative policy. Whereas the former strategy demands incurring some fixed costs associated with the R&D effort, an imitative strategy demands keeping a very competitive cost position, since with little or no advantage in its offer, the business will inevitably be competing on cost. Notice that these postures are basically in conflict so that it is incumbent upon management to select its posture. In many markets, larger business units tend to prefer some modicum of innovation, both to avoid the substantial cash flow consequences of price competition and because of the fact that innovation is largely fixed-cost intensive, so that larger businesses may gain relative advantage from such a strategy. Conversely, smaller firms often prefer imitation, with a leaner and more flexible operation sometimes compensating for scale disadvantages.

KEY STRATEGIC OPTIONS

Grow-Expand Existing Business

This option might be described as a concentric growth strategy, and is well suited to high-potential markets in the early stages of their development. Although they developed at very different rates for good reason, the mass automobile market which arose to greet Ford's Model "T," the instant photography market which grew around Land's Polaroid, or the hand-held calculator market in the state in which Texas Instruments found it upon their entry, all provide examples. In these situations, both product and market mix should be constrained. Faced with large potential markets, currently undeveloped, there is no real need to seek new ones, at least initially. The major concern of the business should be to develop that market. Buyers and potential buyers, as yet relatively unfamiliar with the product, are likely to be less demanding and particular than later in the life-cycle — i.e. the market will be relatively unsegmented. In consequence, the demand for product variety is likely to be relatively muted, and the opportunity for good cost economics correspondingly enhanced. Both demand and supply considerations then, will encourage a focus on expansion of volume, rather than proliferation of product.

Pre-emption of competition should be a major concern of strategy. If this can be done by legal means (patent or otherwise), executives often feel more comfortable. In many instances, however, legal protection is not available, in which case rapid expansion is one of the other alternatives that comes readily to mind. This concern with pre-emption, however, is one of the factors that may lead to consideration of expanding the product-market mix. Even though a decision to add an additional product version or enter a particular market segment may look relatively unprofitable for its own sake, it may be more appropriate for a dominant company to view these initial expansions as a necessary cost of maintaining its position. So often, unfortunately, companies look at these kinds of moves from a narrow financial perspective, and reject them concluding that margins may suffer from the change. A generally more appropriate criterion, however, is "what if" — *what* will this competitor do to my market position and long term profitability *if* we don't take appropriate blocking action now? The basic product/market mix strategy under concentric growth, however, is to keep focused unless forced to broaden by potential or actual competitive incursion.

The aggressiveness with which the business expands its product-market mix has clear implications for innovation policy. More emphasis on growth will typically demand a higher rate of innovation to support product-market mix expansion. If the business was early into the market, much of this innovation must of necessity be self-generated, rather than licensed or "borrowed." In any case, a high level of innovation is typically necessary for defensive reasons alone, if we are positioned in the early stages of a booming growth market.

Rapid expansion, as typically occurs here, tends to consume cash pretty rapidly (see Chapter 4). As a result, the investment demands necessary to support the growth of the existing business are usually so substantial that major changes in vertical integration are unlikely. As the business expands, however, integration should be and will be increased. While contracting out for components and the like often appears attractive as a means of limiting investment during the high-risk start-up phase, once the business is established and management is convinced of the opportunity available, there is increased momentum for internalizing these activities. While this evolutionary approach has much to commend it, it should be noted that this lower risk approach is always vulnerable to the "high roller" competitor willing to pursue higher risk strategies. Thus, faster increases in integration may enable competition to leapfrog a leader, even though they often involve incurring a higher degree of risk.

Grow-Develop New Business

As growth opportunities in core products and markets are seen to be becoming more limited, there is usually, in any case, a tendency to look for other segments and related market opportunities and to begin to expand the product range — what we shall call divergent growth strategies. Some of this broadening of scope, then, is inevitable, and it is often fostered by the emergence of more demanding customers whose needs may become marshalled into market segments. While we have argued, however, that competitive considerations may dictate an early enlargement of scope, it also seems that many businesses fail to build upon their initial success and begin prematurely to explore divergent growth options.

The dangers of excessive expansion of the product-market scope should be clear, for they lie in cost escalation. Serving multiple markets is typically more expansive than serving one, while the economics of long runs of standardized products are typically far superior to those of a broader range. Clearly, then, decisions to expand product/market mix demand careful and accurate cost, price and volume forecasting *ex ante*, as well as careful and dispassionate monitoring *ex post.* It therefore should be most attractive for the majority of manufacturers to look much more closely at further possibilities for convergent or intensive growth options. One is continually struck by the failure of existing manufacturers in a business to identify and group convergent opportunities when they appear. Thus it was not Gottlieb Daimler, or Frederick Lanchester who seized the opportunities for growth in the automobile market, but the Henry Fords, Herbert Austins, and Fritz Opels. The failure of many existing U.S. radio manufacturers to understand the implications of the transistor provides another example. Of course, Ted Levitt might with justification argue that marketing myopia was the primary engine of failure in these examples, but the significance of the point lies in how often technological pioneers fail to perceive and take advantage of market-broadening concentric growth opportunities. In some cases, relatively later entrants pursue these strategies with great success, as the Japanese have done in such diverse industries as motorcycles, 35mm cameras, and portable televisions.[6]

Nonetheless, no matter how great the potential of a market, eventually it provides a successful business with insufficient growth opportunity. Changing either product or market aspects of the mix, however, is fraught with dangers, and many previously successful operations stumble at the transition. The need for new skills and knowledge seems so often underestimated, the necessary up-front costs prove much greater than anticipated, and success-hungry managers often seem to lack the patience necessary to stick with a new venture. Whatever the reason, the scope-broadening ventures of such well-known companies as F.W. Woolworth, Singer, Gillette, EMI and even Honda (early attempts in overseas car markets) provide illustrations of the difficulties.

How, then should businesses go about broadening their product/market mix successfully? Some of the same pointers we discussed in Chapter 4, at the corporate level, also apply. First, look close to home. Growth into related products and related markets is likely to be less risky and to produce earlier returns. Naturally, if insufficient opportunities are available, we must perforce look farther afield. However, both theoretical and empirical arguments support the view that products and markets drastically removed from those in which we are currently operating are likely to portend less beneficial results.[7] Second, be prepared for early setbacks. Patience is important, and early financial returns should not usually be expected. Third, carefully review and attempt to assess objectively the resources which will be needed to exploit these new ventures. The typical tendency seems to be to quantitatively under-estimate the resources that will be necessary, and to qualitatively over-estimate the resources presently "in-house" — a classic example of rose-colored glasses. In addition, there exists a reluctance in some companies to look outside their own company for needed resources and talent. Yet, if the necessary expertise does not currently exist within the company, there may be no timely and sensible alternative.

Again, the now-pressing need to expand mix has implications for both vertical integration and innovation policy. The business will often face difficult allocation decisions — should we, for example, invest to expand our product mix, to integrate backwards into component production or primary processing or to move downstream to secure markets? It is difficult to conceive of scenarios where all such options could or should be pursued simultaneously.

Investment priorities in these difficult cases can, we believe, be derived from the principles basic to the marketing orientation. Namely, make these investments necessary to secure and keep customers *first*, then make others. These precepts translate into policies which place great emphasis on targeting markets and customers first, investing in the products and services necessary to keep those customers second and, finally, looking at integration opportunities that will improve cost and margin performance. The more important integration investments, then, are those that involve securing a source of supply or access to markets, and these fall under our second category above. Note that this approach to setting investment priorities flows directly from the description of the tasks of marketing management we espoused in Chapter 3.

The drive to expand product-market mix will soon begin to outstrip the capability of the original innovators of the business. The increasing demand for new versions of products, and for knowledge about the new markets the business is entering or contemplating implies both expansion and redirection of some key people-intensive activities — which may pose formidable human relations problems. Much of the innovation effort will now be developmental rather than research-intensive — the engineers or designers, if you will, now become more important than the scientists, while maintaining tight control over the quality of new products and timing of the development process will lead to much greater formalization than hitherto. The accompanying influx of new talent, from other businesses or even outside the company, may increase coordination problems and complicate internal politics, but the inexorable demand for new knowledge and approaches demands that the problem be solved in a timely and effective manner. The transition from a business supporting one or a few products to a broad line is a crucial transition, at which many have stumbled. The willingness to acquire and deploy new resources is a crucial prerequisite, but the subsequent demands on the organization, its systems and processes remain high and must be well-managed for successful evolution to occur.

Maintain Volume

Under a maintain volume option, the product/market mix is likely to move into a hold phase — not frozen — but evolving fairly steadily. It will typically be necessary, at a minimum, to match competitors' successful innovations, and to watch carefully for new market segment opportunities. However, a decision to hold back on seeking growth aggressively will mean a shift to much more selective consideration of new product and market opportunities. Indeed, in most cases it will imply a necessity to begin considering elimination of certain products and markets, lest product/market mix expand too much. Note however that if emphasis is placed upon maintaining share, as opposed to volume, then as long as there is some growth left in the overall market of the business we will expect correspondingly less emphasis on elimination and more on product/market mix extension.

With respect to vertical integration strategy, the option of choice will be "maintain." However, a variety of threats may prompt modification of this posture. The three sources of threats are normally viewed as supplier, competitor and customer. However, we must complicate this picture considerably. First, it should be recognized that potential threat is as important as actual threat (indeed, it can be argued that it is more important, since identification of potential threats permits the use of anticipation, facilitating pre-emption or avoidance of actual threat, the principle underlying nuclear arms deterrence policy). Thus our scenario has already expanded, as shown below.

THREAT SCENARIOS

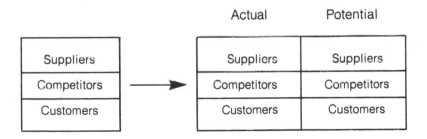

It is a curious commentary on the level of strategic thinking of most managements that whereas their military counterparts (whom they sometimes disparage if not ridicule) have long recognized the need for strategic simulation and game-playing and that, in fact, victories won without fighting are the only kind worth having, thinking pre-emptively seems to be a novel and in many cases resisted concept in business. Presumably the general euphoria created by the growth markets of the sixties and early seventies produced a generation of managers less acute in their competitive thinking. The general scenario since that time seems likely to produce a reaction.

Even this extension, however, is insufficient, for it should be evidence that a potential threat is also afforded by those who seek either our supplies or our customers, albeit for very different reasons. If we are "locked out" of needed crude oil, for example, it will make little difference whether this is done by a chemicals and plastics manufacturer or a fuel hungry airline—we are still stuck with a sizable problem. Similarly, others who sap the purchasing power of our customer may create formidable problems for us—as the auto industry has experienced with its inflation-battered consumers.

In terms of integration threats, then, our prospects may be dimmed not only by forward moves by our suppliers and backward moves by our customers, or by our competitors (in every case, present or potential). They are also affected by forward and backward moves by other agents who share our supply resources or customer base. Finally, government and political risks also pose a threat, particularly if international trade is involved anywhere in our total distribution channel.

In any of these cases, then, we may be forced into integration moves whether we wish to make them or not. Indeed, under the modest investment posture we typically will wish to pursue at this point, it could be argued that we should prefer not to make any integration moves. This would be carrying things too far, however, since consolidation of supply and distribution arrangements is often important in continuing to secure volume. Further, channel arrangements are often in a state of flux and adapting to these changes may also necessitate investment (as in the case of steel service centers, for example) in vertical integration. Thus, it seems wise to advocate a protective or defensive posture with respect to vertical integration, pushing it up where necessary to ensure protection of volume goals, but avoiding it otherwise.

Innovation, however, should still be pursued with vigor. At this point, an external as well as an internal thrust is likely to become more important. Businesses with a history of successful innovation must not permit hardening of the arteries. At the same time, the technology of the business has been disseminating outwards since its inception. It therefore becomes more and more important to scan the external environment broadly for the new modifications and applications to which followers will likely bend the product and/or its technology. With a past history of successful innovation, it is sometimes difficult to avoid developing the "not invented here" (n.i.h.) syndrome — but this is disastrous with broadly disseminated technologies. In other words, willingness to become a licensee (rather than a licensor), to borrow, copy and acquire must all become greater over time if the business wishes to maintain its volume.

Maintain Profit

While size *per se* (measured by size of sales or assets, for example) is important to many managements, to others profit is key. Having already discussed the issue of "profits when?" in Chapter 1, we will avoid that issue for now. Maintaining profits or, even more so, profitability, will be linked with a much more conservative attitude toward product/market scope. Product- and segment-level profitability analysis is an essential management tool at this point. Direct costing systems, always desirable, become one of the necessary prerequisites for successful execution of profit maintenance strategies, for without this information we remain unable to execute.

It is worthwhile noting that many companies back sideways into profit-based strategies after finding that they are expending far too much effort in volume maintenance. Sometimes inability or unwillingness to recognize the evolution in the marketplace plays a part in this phenomenon, while in other cases it takes a major recession and serious losses to lead to the change of strategy. Cynics will argue that many of the prerequisites of professional managers derive from size rather than profits in any case, so that volume maximization will tend to prevail until some rather drastic event forces change.[8]

As focus shifts from volume to profit, however, management begins casting a much more critical eye on the operations of the business. Some rationalization of product — market scope is almost inevitable at this point, certainly if the business had been in a volume-maintenance mode previously. Careful analysis of product sales and profitability, including such considerations as demand cross-elasticity, while not being deluded by allocations of overhead, will typically lead to candidates for deletion or, short of this, significant price increases (which may speed the decision to delete unless earlier pricing policies were erroneous). Comparable analysis of market segments and customers will likely lead to similar options of deletion and price increases. In addition, over time there is often a tendency for breakeven order sizes to move upwards, so that minimum volumes per order and/or per time period must often be adjusted when profit becomes primary. Thus, it may often be the case that volume falls away as profit emphasis increases. This is not necessarily bound to occur, however, since some of the effort previously devoted to less profitable products and customers may be redeployed in ways that increase not only profits but volume too. Nonetheless, if profitability (e.g. Return on Sales [ROS] or Return on Investment [ROI]) becomes more important than total profit, then volume loss is almost inevitable.

Investment policy must now become much more stringent and selective. Whereas under volume/share maintenance incremental investments to match competitors' new products would typically be made, under profit maintenance they may not be. On the other hand investments in process technology and product redesign aimed at cost reduction are very important, and the focus of our R & D effort is therefore on cost reduction and process improvements that in turn will lead to cost reduction.

Vertical integration moves will now be much more limited. Whereas, under volume maintenance, backward and forward moves may often be justified on defensive grounds — *viz.* the need to protect markets and supplies — this is now a rather specious argument. Instead, the criterion is profit, and the decisions on further integration are more likely to be negative. Changes will most likely be incremental, unless a major distribution catastrophe is threatened, or a profitable integration opportunity falls into our laps like manna from heaven.

As profit takes precedence, manning policy and overhead levels should come under close scrutiny. The typical response to the halcyon days of growth of the business is featherbedding, not only in terms of poor labor practices for hourly workers, with overly generous agreements and rigid productivity-limiting work rules quite common, but also at the management level where top-heavy management and unproductive staff are bogging the business down and imposing disproportionate cost penalties. Thus, cost analysis of the whole management structure now comes into play, and the paring of overhead costs, redeployment of labor and demanning by attrition, early retirement plans or retrenchment will be common.

In summary, then, profit maintenance is likely to lead to a much more stringent operating environment. Product — market mix will narrow, and volume may fall away. Investment policy will be cautious and conservative, and integration moves very limited.

Harvest Strategy

Whereas volume may be maintained or even somewhat increased under the previous option, depending upon what is necessary to maintain or increase profits, the harvest option represents a clear decision to shrink the size of the business. In addition, the primary criterion for assessing business performance has now shifted from profits to cash flow, a shift which has wide-ranging consequences. If these consequences are recognized, and the harvest decision made explicitly, then management is basically doing its strategic job. Often, however, companies begin to harvest by default. The search for regular profits is obviously ongoing, but note that it is but a short step from extreme profit-consciousness to the point where management begins to shrink the business, where even the minimally necessary defensive innovation is sacrificed on the altar of profit. Obviously, it is hard to warm to the idea that objectives and strategy should emerge by default, even though this sometimes occurs, and we would argue strongly for avoiding this error.

With primary focus on cash flow, incremental investment will typically be avoided. Assuming the business has a reasonable future life ahead of it, however (e.g. market conditions are mature but not in drastic decline), certain capital expenditures may be made. For example, for the business to continue to generate cash over a reasonable period of time, operating costs must be kept reasonably competitive. If they begin to rise relative to competition, cash flow will ultimately be compromised by competitors taking price leadership. Unfortunately, it is always tempting to defer this kind of expenditure to improve shorter term cash flows. In many companies, also, the habit of evaluating performance *versus* last year or budget (a very inward-oriented perspective) instead of *versus* competitors may lead to a situation where costs become considerably out of line with competitors before management wakes up to the fact. Here, then, cash flows are typically impeded, and rather than being faced with a series of smaller incremental expenditures, management is faced with a large and traumatic decision involving either large expenditures or exit. Rather than reaping a harvest, we reap a whirlwind.

Recognizing, then, that there may sometimes exist the necessity for some kind of investment in the harvest mode, we should also note that we should avoid it wherever possible. In general, we should be working to lower our fixed costs, while keeping variable costs competitive. SPI suggests the best combination is often the newest equipment in the oldest building, because this should give lower fixed and variable costs. However, the main point is that we do not want to raise our breakeven point nor our operating leverage when in harvest mode. Indeed, any cost-saving investment predicated upon either higher levels of output (operations) or even maintaining high stable levels of output should now be avoided, since it is now possible that industry demand and/or our demand will be diminishing in the future. These general policies will have enormous impact on vertical integration strategy, for the desirability of lowering the extent of integration now becomes very clear. First, liquidation of upstream and downstream assets not related to the core of the operations of the business may augment cash flows. In addition, such moves will typically enable management to variate more of the cost structure of the business, lowering its breakeven point.

Finally, once the shrink decision is made, innovation will be cut to a bare minimum. If the industry is one where cross-licensing is common (which tends to occur more where there is *not* yet global competition), the business may eliminate any internal R & D and instead "listen" for new technology that might be licensed to improve cash performance.

Exit Strategy

Getting out gracefully seems never as easy to do as to say. For many businesses, however, this process can be greatly facilitated by divesting to competitors who will be continuing in the business. Often, low market share businesses in declining markets will be the first candidates to elect exit. Some remaining competitors who feel their prospects or the market's are better will be prime prospects for making the acquisition. Generally speaking weaker competitors are well advised to seek earlier exit, since by doing so they can often avoid liquidation, avoid a write-off and even make relatively profitable exits.

One of the major reasons why many businesses find it much more attractive to exit by divestiture rather than liquidation involves different problems that may arise in dealing with such issues as service and guarantee contracts, product liability requirements and severance payments. Unfortunately, high growth and profitability are usually accompanied by laxity and it is often not until late stages in the maturity cycle of the business that the full cost of earlier years of lax management are seen. A business will usually be much better positioned for exit if management recognized from its beginning that such a possibility existed — but many managements act as though it did not!

Failing divestiture, another possibility which may ease the withdrawal by reducing severance costs for management and/or labor is to consider a management and/or worker buyout. So called leveraged buyouts, with investment bankers providing the capital, have become quite common in the United States, and offer attractive possibilities to the seller and the new ownership. Workers' cooperatives are a more common solution in Europe than in the U.S., but labor unions often become heavily involved in the restructuring efforts of the existing company. Management or worker buyouts can be a disastrous recipe, however, for the partial exit decision. To permit one or some of several facilities in a multiplant operation to fall into the hands of existing management or labor will often unleash another low-cost competitor to worsen competitive conditions, while keeping in operation capacity which would usually be best shut down from the perspective of industry prices and returns.

Finally, of course, we are faced with shutdown or liquidation of the business. Always a painful decision to make, it is often even more painful to implement. Even though the restructuring options may arouse some interest on the part of management, there are few managers who savor the prospect of being the hatchet man. Further, many of them are ill-suited to the task—not just for emotional reasons—but also because they lack the necessary skills. The use of expert assistance is therefore very worth considering at this point. In the longer term, large companies would be well advised to foster the development of these skills. Many companies go out of their way to nurture the skills and talents involved in successfully launching and managing new ventures. Yet, in a world of faster product life cycles and evolving technological diversity, turnover of products is likely to increase. The inevitable consequence is that firms will more frequently be involved in product and business phaseouts and shutdowns in the future. Going out gracefully has many benefits, which are not by any means solely economical. Bethlehem Steel, nursing a $255 million loss and significant unpopularity as a result of closing its Lackawanna, New York plant, is one of the many companies that have found the barriers to exit truly formidable.!

SUMMARY AND CONCLUSIONS

In this chapter, we have reviewed the basic issues which must be resolved in developing business unit strategy. We focussed first upon defining the business itself, and isolating its mission. We then discussed establishing the strategic direction of the business, and the major broad options which exist. The next section reviewed three key strategic decision areas, involving product-market mix, vertical integration and innovation. We then discussed the evolution of business unit strategy over time, through its major stages from the growth through the exit options.

As we noticed in Chapter 4 when discussing corporate strategy, much of the concern in developing good business strategies also is focussed upon managing the mix of products and markets and, in this case, its evolution over time. Good coordination is always important, but while substantial mix extension and modification is occurring, the links among marketing (or sales), R & D and engineering (or design) and manufacturing (or operations) are extremely important. Still today, in too many companies, the linkages between marketing and market inputs and the innovation process are either nonexistent or far too weak. The notion that a business strategy can be both good and, at the same time, bereft of marketing content is inconceivable. Unless marketing managers reassert themselves in the business planning process, it is likely that poor business strategies will continue to emerge from the strategic planning efforts of many firms, with poor performance and missed objectives the inevitable consequence.

REFERENCES AND FOOTNOTES

1. J. G. March and H. A. Simon, *Organizations*, New York: John Wiley, 1958.

2. Alfred D. Chandler, *Strategy and Structure*, Cambridge, Mass.: MIT Press, 1962.

3. Abell, in a normative approach, argues for three key elements of customers, need and technology. This is insufficient descriptively, even though one may agree with the author's normative view. See Derek F. Abell, *Defining the Business*, Englewood Cliffs, N.J.: Prentice-Hall, 1980.

4. Theodore Levitt, "Marketing Myopia," *Harvard Business Review*, July-August 1960, pp. 45-56.

5. James Brian Quinn, *Strategies for Change*, Homewood, Ill.: Richard D. Irwin, 1980.

6. For a description of Honda's success in motor cycles see Thomas M. Hout, Michael E. Porter and Eileen Rudden, "How Global Companies Win Out," *Harvard Business Review*, Vol. 60, September-October 1982, pp. 98-108.

7. The work of Ansoff and Rumelt, referred to in Chapter 4, would support this argument.

8. The economists have devoted some considerable attention to this issue. See William J. Baumol, *Business Behavior, Value and Growth*, New York: Macmillan, 1959.

6

FORMULATING
THE PRODUCT

MARKET STRATEGY

As we have seen, strategy exists at many levels within a company, and this is no doubt partly responsible for the confusion which often exists with respect to the function of a strategy, its elements, and the part which strategy plays in the planning process. In this chapter, we focus on the level which is most important for marketing planning purposes, namely the product market level. We shall direct our discussion to the development of a marketing strategy for a product being sold into a particular market. In doing so, we shall clarify both the purposes and content of a marketing strategy, and we shall deal in detail with the specific elements which should comprise a sound statement of a product market strategy. We shall also attempt to distinguish clearly among objectives, strategies, and tactics, as well as to illustrate the natural linkages which should exist among the various elements of a well designed strategy.

THE FUNCTION OF A STRATEGY

The fundamental function of any strategy is to provide the manager with direction on where and how to manage an area of the business during a future period, whether it be one, three, five years or longer. The product market level of planning is the key building block or cell for purposes of developing marketing strategy, and it is providing direction for that entity upon which we now focus. There are three requirements which must be met, however, if the strategy is to prove workable. Each of these is now examined.

Achieving Coordination

To provide useful direction, an effective strategy must ensure that managers from various departments or units within an organization are all working with the same goal in mind. Thus, a good strategy must also coordinate and integrate the various functions which are involved in the achievement of that strategy. Because the requirements of each market or segment are unique (Chapter 3) it is vital that this integration be achieved at the product market level. The example below illustrates this point.

Suppose that in the role of the division general manager, we asked the division's sales manager what steps he or she might take to improve profits for a particular product. While some sales managers might respond that they need to reduce expenses; many would suggest that they need

- A larger sales force
- More advertising
- Better incentives for distributors
- Better quality products
- Faster delivery
- More flexible credit policies
- New products
- Flexible pricing systems

Many of these steps will increase costs, either for the manufacturing or the sales department, but these can be justified through the resulting higher volume of sales. Thus, the sales manager sees the route to profits through greater sales volume.

Suppose we then turned to the manufacturing director and asked what he or she might do to improve the profitability of the product. In this case we might see suggestions along the following lines:

- A reduced number of products in order to facilitate longer production runs

- Easier delivery schedules (accommodating manufacturing schedules)

- Moratorium on new products (which typically cause problems in the startup phase)

- Less concern over quality of the products

- Better forecasting of sales

- Installation of new equipment design to improve productivity.

If we now asked the R and D director for his advice on improving profits he would likely respond that with more time a product could be developed which is far superior to any currently on the market. Of course, this product will require more funds to finish the final stages of development. If we talk to our director of human resources, the response will often be that we need to hire better people, to do more training of those people whom we already employ, and that we need to develop an improved compensation and benefits package.

Of course, the finance director will typically have a different response. His concern will usually focus on ways to improve the return on investment, either by increasing profits (increasing prices or reducing expenses) or by a decrease in the assets of the business (fixed or working capital). Thus, when the finance director is asked for approval on new capital expenses, the response is typically "No, the proposal requires further justification."

Although the above may appear to smack of parody, the fact is that there is potential for severe conflict and discord between the key functional directors of most organizations. Each manager is seeking to perform in a way which seems most appropriate for his or her position, based upon individual backgrounds and training, as well as existing reward structures. Very often, sales managers desire to sell more, manufacturing to reduce costs, R & D to develop the ultimate quality in product, human resources to improve people quality and finance to improve the budget or control long term expenditures. Indeed, depending on how these responsibilities are executed, it could even be argued that to pursue these goals means no more than that functional managers are doing their jobs.

To develop a direction, however, these conflicts must be resolved. In most companies the solution to the conflict comes through compromise. Through the use of committees, political power, or asking top management for a decision, a compromise is often reached. Whereas the compromise solution usually placates each manager to some degree, there is great danger that consensus will be reached based upon internal considerations rather than external. If this is the case, the winner is not the firm as a whole, but our competitors. If competitors are more sensitive to the needs of customers, they will come to the market with an offer which is better tuned to the marketplace. When this occurs, there is little consolation from the fact that we have resolved our internal battles, for we will have lost the key battle for customers.

Our example might make it appear that each manager is being parochial or short sighted, by focussing almost exclusively on his or her specific function or department. It is important to remember, however, that organizations around the world often evaluate and reward their managers for behaving as depicted above. Sales managers are encouraged to reach sales quotas; manufacturing directors to run efficient plants; research directors to design better products; human resources and personnel directors to up-grade personnel quality (while cutting labor costs) and finance directors to improve profitability particularly by limiting new investments. So often, however, these traditional standards and criteria are out of kilter with what is necessary to beat competitors and win customers. The key, then is to ensure that we build a genuine consensus around the direction embodied in the strategy, and to attempt to ensure that the reward system and eval-uation criteria that are used are congruent with the expectations of the strategies being developed.

Obviously, then, a strategy which is not accepted, is poorly articulated or not well understood, cannot help in improving coordination. To have a strategy, however, is a necessary, if not sufficient, condition for building momentum in a given direction. A useful way to think about its role, is to visualize it as the yoke or harness, for just as this keeps oxen or horses pull-ing as a team, so too does a strategy act as a yoke or collar around the necks of managers to keep them from pulling in opposite directions. This yoke is not designed to stifle creativity or activity but to ensure that all im-portant functions involved in contributing to the product-market strategy are moving in the same direction.

Allocating Scarce Resources

The second requirement which must be met by any strategy statement — corporate, business or product-market level — is closely linked with the need to coordinate and integrate the functions described above. At any level of the organization resources are limited. Strategy must define in a clear yet general way how those scarce resources are to be allocated. If we define objectives as the ends we wish to achieve, then strategy is about al-locating scarce resources in such a way that will help us achieve those ends. Indeed, very often some resource, whether it be manufacturing capacity, sales force time, money, technology or something else, will be more limiting than others. In many organizations, these limitations are seen most acutely when resources are shared — e.g., manufacturing capacity is scarce because we share it with another division. The lower we go in the organization, the more resources are typically shared. Thus, paradoxically perhaps, strategy is absolutely essential at the product-market cell level, where we must have clear guidance on how to allocate the scarce resources. In the case of the sale force, for example, time is usually a key constraint. A sales strategy, then, should suggest how the sales force should be allocating its time over the various customers and products for which it is responsible. Clearly, strategy is most important for the most limiting resource, but since all are scarce, is necessary for all.

Later in the chapter, we shall describe more fully the development of strategy at the product market level. Yet it should already be evident that if resources are scarce and there are competing demands upon them, in any attempt to allocate them we are thrown again into the pit of conflict we discussed in the previous section. By what means should we attempt to clearly specify how resources will be allocated, achieving integrated and coordinated effort *without* imposing disharmony and conflict upon the organization and its members? Perhaps in Japan, with its reputation for harmonious relationships and organizational allegiances, this task might prove less difficult, but in many Western economies it poses formidable problems. We cannot be equivocal if we wish a clear strategy to emerge, yet to develop and agree upon this direction calls for skills in the management process of building true consensus — seldom a quick fix but nonetheless vitally important. Yet this consensus must be built upon a sound and realistic view of the customer. Without this, we shall not meet the third requirement of a good strategy — upon which we now focus.

Beating Competition

Our last requirement is that we recognize that any strategy, to be effective, must show how we can beat our competitors. Indeed, some would argue that the key function of a strategy is to enable us to win over our competitors. Yet it is curious that so many marketing managers seem to act as though they had no competition. Too frequently we see failure to make any explicit assessment of potential competitor response in formulating strategies. Sometimes, strategy statements read as if the competitor will ignore not only our actions, but better yet leave the market when we enter. These are, of course, very rare responses. An analogy to playing chess helps to illustrate the point. A chess player soon learns that in order to defeat an opponent, he or she must think several moves in advance. Going further, however, master chess players often attempt to think through the entire game from initial move to final checkmate. The need for this approach is very real. The player knows that by his moving to a certain spot, the competitor will have a discrete number of moves, many of them predictable. The second, third, and all subsequent moves will attempt to move against the competitor so as to reduce the competitor's number of options. If done with skill, each move serves to reduce these options until the opponent must capitulate. In professional sports and, as we have mentioned, the military arena, tremendous efforts are expended on studying and analyzing "competitors" indicating again the lessons to be learned by managers engaged in oligopolistic competition.

In business, of course, we are not necessarily seeking the capitulation or annihilation of our competitor. We are, however, seeking to reduce the number of options open to the competitor, particularly those which might enable him to attack our vulnerabilities. Thus, although the number of moves open to competitors are far greater than in chess, our strategies must attempt, *a priori*, to consider likely responses. Any strategy which will not withstand reasonably probable competitor responses should be rejected. Those which enable us to beat our competitor are worthy of further consideration. Such further consideration might involve developing contingent responses to alternative competitive scenarios, and — in effect — laying out second or even third moves which we might make. While these options may not end up in formal contingency plans, *per se*, they should give us higher quality strategies as well as the ability to act pre-emptively.

To make this requirement more operation requires that any strategy we develop possess at least one of the four attributes listed below. If possible, the strategy should commit us to action which our competitor *cannot* duplicate. Whether it is because of financial or technological limitations, lack of plant capacity, lesser coverage or even a less established reputation in the market, or some other reason, a strategy in other respects good which our competitor *cannot* execute affords us an excellent opportunity for beating him. Somewhat less desirable is a strategy which competitors could match if they chose to, but one which we can be assured they will *not choose* to adopt. Naturally, to be confident requires considerable insight into competitors' management. Perhaps our past experience with them has convinced us they will not choose this option. Alternatively, we may recognize that they are putting their money behind other products or they do not want to besmirch their image or hurt their cash flow by dropping price. By whatever means, however, we must convince ourselves that they will not decide to replicate our strategy. The third possibility is that we predict that they will follow our strategic moves. It may be that we have still found a good strategy, for our competitor may be *relatively disadvantaged* by such a move. For example, in an inelastic market, should a competitor with a large market share decide to follow our across-the-board price cut, their larger volume will result in a greater opportunity loss in the short term. Conversely, should a small competitor try to match a large competitor's fixed-cost expenditures in R & D, market coverage, advertising, technical services or breadth of product line, he will generally suffer relative to the larger competitor, who can more easily recover these fixed costs over his greater number of units. The fourth option is the situation where a move by us would result in benefits to us as well as our competitors. For example, an increase in price which results in an immediate matching by our competitors or a decrease in service or advertising expenditure which is matched by our competitors are examples of situations where all competitors might improve profitability as a result of our strategies. Here, we would seek strategies which yielded the greatest *relative advantage* to ourselves.

ELEMENTS OF THE PRODUCT/MARKET STRATEGY

A product/market strategy contains the following eight elements:

- strategic objectives
- operational objectives
- selection of strategic alternatives(s)
- choice of customer targets
- choice of competitor targets
- selection of core strategy
- description of supporting marketing mix programs
- description of supporting functional mix programs

The first three elements, strategic and operational objectives and choice of strategic alternatives establish the broad goals and directions for the product/market strategy. The second three elements, the customer, the customer and competitor targets, and the core strategy, sometimes known as the three c's of marketing strategy, determine the postioning of the product in the market.[1] The last two sets of elements, the supporting marketing and functional mix requirements deal with the tactics or programs which will be necessary to successfully implement the strategy. They lay out in a general way the parameters of the broad action steps needed from various departments or functions to ensure that the planned strategy will be executed. Thus, after the objectives and broad strategy are determined and the positioning established, implementation must come through the actions of many people throughout the organization. This is what we meant earlier when we said that the strategy must provide the coordination and integrating theme if we are to achieve our objectives.

Choosing the Strategic Objective

Choice of the strategic objective is one of the most fundamental decisions for any product or market. It establishes the results that we wish to attain during the planning period. Broadly, strategic objectives may be grouped into three broad categories, encompassing profitability, cash flow, and growth objectives. Before the strategy process can proceed, the manager must determine which of these three broad categories of objectives is of greatest concern for a particular time frame. Although some guidance may come from above, it is vital that the marketing manager *also* addresses this key issue. He must decide, for example, whether growth (in terms of sales volume or market share) is of greater concern than profitability (in terms of margins or return on investment) over the relevant planning period. While the objective will usually change over a longer time range — and this is quite appropriate — for any particular time period, a choice must be made. This is necessary because maximum growth, maximum profitability and maximum cash flow are incompatible objectives in the short term. We simply cannot have the best of all worlds all at once, whereas in the long term, growth today, profitability two years hence, and positive cash flow four years hence may be both eminently attainable and a wise set of objectives.

Figure 6-1 illustrates how these objectives might well change as a product goes through its life cycle. In its early stages (when the product is a problem child or star in BCG terminology) the objective is generally to grow with or faster than the market growth. As the rate of market growth begins to decline and/or our market share is considered sufficient, we might choose to improve profit margins or the return on investment. As the life cycle proceeds toward the maturity stage and decline appears imminent, concern for cash flow is likely to predominate. Although these guidelines are not meant as cast-iron prescriptions for the choice of a strategic objective, they do reflect what many companies appear to be doing if we can infer that the business results are reflective of their objectives. Table 6-1, derived from the PIMS study described earlier, shows how the financial and marketing results of businesses vary as they move through their life cycles. These numbers represent averages of more than one thousand businesses over a four year period. The figures illustrate how the growth of sales and market share are high in the early stages and lower in the later stages of the life cycle. Return on investment and cash flow, however, which were negative in the early stage became positive later in the life cycle.

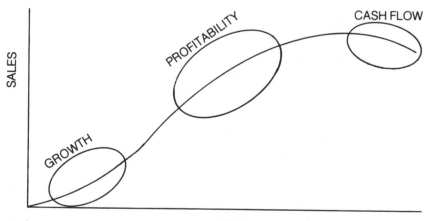

FIGURE 6-1 Evolution of Strategic Objectives

TABLE 6-1 Operating Results of PIMS Businesses*

LIFE CYCLE STAGE

CATEGORY	MEASURE	START-UP	GROWTH	EARLY MATURITY	LATE MATURITY
Market Performance	-Sales Growth	74	21	12	8
	-Market Share	8	24	25	22
Budget Levels	-R & D/Sales	10	3	2	1
	-Marketing/Sales	26	10	10	8
Financial Performance	-ROI	-19	22	22	18
	-Net Income Growth	7	20	15	11
	-Investment Growth	38	16	9	6
	-CF/Investment	-46	-2	4	4

Source: The Strategic Planning Institute

*Data are four-year average percentages, except growth rates which are annual rates in current dollars.

Data appearing in Column 1 (Start-Up) are medians.

Whatever the choice of strategic objective, this decision is central to the decisions which follow. Because it is such a critical choice, both top management and division or SBU management will typically exert a fair amount of influence over the choice. It is also vital that the managers closely involved with the product or market area — typically marketing or product managers — also be involved. The decision on objectives, then, should ideally have all key managers involved, and the decision should be predicated upon a thorough situation analysis of the product/market. Using all the information available, the group of managers can thus participate and come to a solution which, in the ideal case, will not be based upon compromise but upon their best judgments about the direction that the business should be taking. Top management must provide the direction for the division or business unit, but at the product/market level, the inclusion of key managers will help to build the consensus. The Japanese management system has been far more successful in this approach than have the approaches of many American and European firms. By including the relevant managers in building the consensus for this critical decision, greater commitment is created. It is crucial to avoid the pattern prevalent in some American companies where the marketing or strategic planning department will develop a plan which it thinks is most logical, only to see it sabotaged by other departments that did not "buy in" to the chosen strategy.

Operational Objectives

The distinction between the strategic and operational objective is one of specificity. Whereas the strategic objective establishes the general direction for the product or market, the operational objective provides the numbers which tell how much, when, and in some cases, where. First, an operational objective must specify the amount of sales volume or market share, profit margin or cash flow that is to be targeted. In a strategic plan this figure should be specified for each of the three or five years of the plan, and, as we noted earlier, the relative emphasis upon particular strategic objectives may change dramatically during the period of the strategic plan. The *when* question is also answered by specifying the amounts for time period, typically by quarter for an annual marketing plan, by year for a strategic plan. The question of *where* refers to the situation where a strategy covers several market segments. In this instance, the objective should be set for each market segment such as geographical regions or industry groupings. For a range of products, operational objectives will also be set for each version.

The purpose of operational objectives is straightforward: to provide a specific goal or end result for all managers as a group to achieve and to offer a means of measurement and control to see whether this goal is being or has been achieved. It is necessary, therefore, to provide a benchmark figure at the outset of the time period so that some means of measurement is possible. It is critical that these objectives be challenging to the managers as a group while still being realistic. Objectives which are beyond the reach of managers act more as a disincentive or "demotivator" rather than as a positive motivator. The key word to keep in mind is *operational*—we are providing standards for evaluation as well as concrete measurable targets toward which to direct our efforts.

Selection of Strategic Alternatives

The choice of a strategic alternative(s) follows in large measure from our choice of a strategic objective. This does not imply that the decision is easy, but instead that strategic alternatives must be chosen so as to be in concert with strategic objectives. Strategic alternatives are really the first step in strategy (as opposed to objective) development. If where we stand today is point A, and where we wish to be (objective) is point B, then the strategic alternatives we will pursue may be thought of as the broad road map from point A to point B, the major route we shall follow. Of course, an enormous amount of work remains in fleshing out our strategy, but the framework we shall now describe has the enormous advantage of helping us clarify our thinking about the broad course of action or the direction that we should follow.

Figure 6-2 shows a means-ends chain illustrating the linkages between strategic objectives and strategic alternatives. To most managers, improving the profits or profitability of a business is the most important overall long term goal for any product or market. There are at least two broad pathways to improve profits, however; to increase the sales volume, or to become more productive and thereby improve the cash flow from the business. Looking therefore at the top two levels of Figure 6-2, we find a relationship to the three strategic objectives discussed earlier. Thus the objective of improving profits or profitability can come through two broad or general strategic alternatives of increased sales volume or increased productivity. Beneath each of these, however, are more specific alternatives.

Increasing Productivity

Moving from right to left in Figure 6-2 we find that productivity is defined as a ratio of output to input. Thus, increased productivity can come either through increased outputs, at this point not related to sales volume, or by reducing the inputs incurred in generating a given sales volume.

Two strategic alternatives are open to us should we wish to increase the

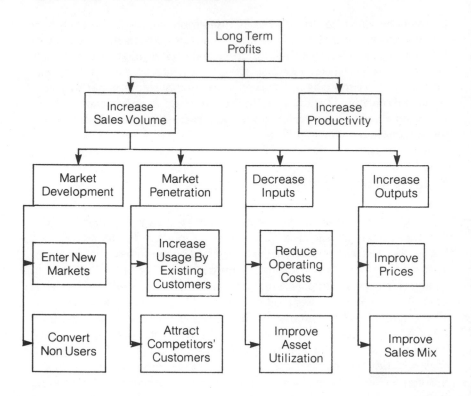

FIGURE 6-2 Developing Strategic Alternatives

dollar volume from current unit sales. The easiest approach is to improve prices. We may execute this alternative in a wide variety of ways — for example by increasing the list price, reducing discounts, reducing trade allowances, etc. Alternatively we may seek to improve the mix of sales. We might do this by changing the product mix so that we sell more of our more profitable products and less of our less profitable ones, or by changing the customer mix of sales to deemphasize less profitable customers. Again, there are many different ways to execute either of these alternatives.

The reduction of inputs to increase efficiency and thus cash flow is more obvious. Cost reduction possibilities may be widespread in such areas as advertising, sales force, training programs, manufacturing costs, distribution expenses, and so on, and opportunities will probably exist to cut elements of both fixed and variable costs. The second alternative refers to the improvement of asset utilization or, if you will, to cut the financial costs of doing business. Most marketing managers are involved with the management of two forms of market assets which can be controlled: inventories and accounts receivable. In times of high interest rates or economic decline for example, there is often significant pressure from the finance department to reduce inventories and receivables across the board. While such measures may be necessary, we are here suggesting a more selective approach to the management of these assets. Obviously, however, if we can cut the amount of money invested in current assets, we reduce both the cash investment as well as the interest cost (implied or otherwise) on this investment — moves which increase both the cash flow and the profitability of the business.

Taking these four strategic alternatives as a group, we find that they can help to improve profitability in two ways. In financial terms, profitability can be improved in two major ways:

$$\text{Return on Assets} = \frac{\text{Profits}}{\text{Assets}} = \frac{\text{Profits}}{\text{Sales}} \times \frac{\text{Sales}}{\text{Assets}}$$

$$= \text{Profit Margin} \times \text{Asset Turnover}$$

The first three steps that we discussed, improving sales mix, price, and cost reduction refer to a direct increase in the profit margins for the product or market. The last step, improving asset utilization, results from an increase in asset turnover. Profitability can be improved through either means. Some firms like retail institutions make a very low profit margin but their turnover is high. Other highly capital-intensive businesses may have a turnover of 1.0 or less, but their profit margins should be relatively higher. Thus, we have several strategic alternatives open to us if our primary strategic objective is to increase the productivity or efficiency of this area of the business. These are strategic alternatives often employed for more mature businesses, where cash flow is a key concern.

Increase Volume

The broad strategies to increase sales volume are also divided into two categories in Figure 6-2: the development of new markets and the further penetration of markets in which we are already active. The development of new markets is again broken into two categories: entering new markets and converting nonusers of the product in existing segments.

Entering new markets or segments where we as a company have not sought to sell in the past might include such options as geographical expansion or seeking new customer groups based on demographics or socioeconomics. A Japanese company deciding to sell in Brazil, or Johnson and Johnson seeking to sell baby powder for use by adults in addition to babies would be good examples. Although the market or segment may already exist, we treat it as a new market because for us as a competitor it is new and we must develop an entire marketing campaign unlike the strategies currently used in existing segments.

The converting of nonusers in existing segments is a subtle differentiation, but one which we think is important for designing effective strategies. In this we and our direct competitors may have been trying to sell to these potential customers for some time, but they do not buy from our competitors or us. In one sense they are already part of our potential market, but for one reason or another they are not using the type of product that we or our direct competitors offer. Examples include the decision of a farmer not to use agricultural herbicides but to rely on nonchemical methods; the decision of a small business not to use a business computer but to continue to rely on a manual bookkeeping system used for many years; a decision of a consumer not to purchase an instant camera but to continue using a camera which requires photoprocessing. In essence these customers prefer to use a different technology or not to be involved with any supplier in the product class of which we are a part. We categorize this as a developmental alternative because our strategies need to consider these customers almost as new markets rather than as people already familiar with our product class. In one sense we might say that the market has passed these people by in that the product might be mature in existing markets, but these potential customers have never tried the product and thus need to be developed just as the market was developed originally. In most countries there is still a significant number of people who have never flown in an airplane for tourist or business reasons, but who represent a potential market. This potential market may be very small or too expensive to develop, particularly if the segment is fairly mature and penetration of potential is high, but it represents a segment which must be treated differently. Often the first-time flier needs to be reassured about safety of an airplane, for example, more than the frequency of the schedules or comfort of the seats.

Market penetration alternatives are also separated into two classes: to increase the rate of usage of the product class among existing customers, and to attract customers away from our competitors. In both cases the customer is already using the class of product which we offer.

To encourage increased usage we might enlarge the unit of purchase, increase the rate of obsolescence, find new uses for our product, or provide price incentives to purchase larger quantities. This is a common strategy in consumer products where we observe advertising which suggests that Jello can be used for a salad as well as desserts, that orange juice can be used for meals other than breakfast, that Coca-Cola can be used as a mix with various kinds of alcoholic beverages and so on. Among industrial products, customers might be encouraged to increase its uses for a computer or the number of applications for a particular material. The advantage of this general alternative is that the customer is already familiar with the product class and frequently with our product as well. The alternative of attracting competitors' customers is the predominant option implicit or explicit in most strategies. This option assumes that we and our direct competitors are fighting for the same customer, one who is already familiar with the product class but is using our competitor's product, either exclusively or predominantly. It often appears to offer opportunities for a quick increase in sales, sometimes at the expense of price or service, but it is the option to which the competitor is most likely to retaliate and to do so promptly.

Among the four strategic alternatives to increase sales volume, the entering of new market segments is most risky for companies not particularly strong in marketing. Lack of knowledge of the marketplace and inability to understand new markets are often grounds for failure. The converting of nonusers can be an attractive option if the market is sufficiently large and willing to change, primarily because the competitors are often avoiding these segments. Increasing the usage rate is very attractive particularly where customers are pleased with our products and service. Attracting competitors' customers is a good short-term solution but can often be expensive, particularly in slow growth markets where lowering the price becomes a means to steal more customers.

In summary, Figure 6-2 shows four basic ways of increasing sales volume and four basic ways to improve productivity, and thus cash flow. Having identified the alternatives, however, we now must make a difficult decision. Among these alternatives we must choose one or perhaps two where we can concentrate our efforts. The danger of seeing the alternatives is to assume that because all are quite attractive, they should all be pursued with equal vigor. It is all too common to attempt too much, and this can so easily lay the grounds for subsequent failure. Our scarce resources must be carefully focused, for therein lies the art of strategy. If we fail to do so, we shall find ourselves pursuing mutually contradictory activities — not uncommon perhaps, but scarcely the concerted and coordinated direction we said should be provided by our strategy. The principle of selectivity and concentration, which we discussed in Chapter 3, can be deployed to great advantage in seeking a focus among the strategic alternatives.

Positioning Strategy

The term market position gives the impression that the market planner has chosen a specific physical spot in which to place his or her products. Its marketing connotations are, however, broader. The term is used quite loosely by consumer marketers, who talk about "positioning," such products as soaps, toothpaste and other consumer products. In fact, developing a positioning strategy for a product involves key decisions with respect to customers, competitors and the benefits to be offered. These are reflected in the next three elements of the product market strategy which we shall discuss:

- choice of customer targets

- choice of competitor targets

- choice of a core strategy or incentive for the customer to buy our product

Each of these decisions is highly interrelated with the others, but we must perforce discuss them sequentially.

Choice of Customer Targets

The typical first step in developing the positioning strategy is to select the customer target. As we noted in Chapter 3, most markets are comprised of segments, and — given that markets have already been chosen in the corporate or SBU strategy — we now focus on the segments for which we wish to compete. One basic issue that must be dealt with is the number of segments in which we shall compete. In some cases, corporate or business strategy will leave little scope for decision at this level (see Chapter 5), but in other cases this issue may yet remain unresolved.

We must also choose the specific segment(s) we shall target. A variety of criteria may be used to assist with this task, and basic measures such as size, growth rate and anticipated profitability that we have already discussed (Chapter 4) are often used to facilitate this process. Competitive considerations should also enter in, since it may otherwise be difficult to avoid choosing the largest segment as our target. Obviously other competitors may also do so, leading to what one of our colleagues calls the "majority fallacy." In these conditions, smaller segments less subject to competitive entreaty may ultimately prove much more attractive.

In addition, we must also decide at which level in the channel of distribution we should be targeting the bulk of our marketing effort. We discuss this issue at greater length in Chapter 7, but it should be evident that we always face this type of problem. Should we, for example, direct most of our effort to the trade or distribution *vis-a-vis* the end consumer? Or, if we are an industrial company, should we direct our efforts to the distributors who purchase from us or the end user who is their customer? We can rarely afford to apply equally high effort at all levels, nor is this necessarily a wise strategy, so that we typically end up with one level which receives the largest effort—the primary customer target—and others which receive less—the secondary targets, if you will.

In organizational buying situations, we must also carefully analyze the various decision influences to target our effort well. In export marketing, Japanese capital goods producers have developed an excellent reputation for casting a broad net in terms of influencers, by intensive selling efforts at multiple levels, broadly spread through the buying organization. In markets where a few large buying organizations are important, the targeting effort should obviously be very precise, based upon analysis of specific customer accounts and the individuals within them. As we noted in Chapter 3, it is vital that we avoid the often fatal flaw of defining the customer too narrowly, and analyze the various roles—be they specifier, influencer, user etc. — involved in the buy-use-rebuy cycle.

Key information needed to help define customer targets also includes their needs—i.e., the benefits they are seeking and/or the problems they wish to solve—and, of course, their identity (individual or aggregate) so that we might communicate our offer to them.

Choice of Competitor Targets

"Competitor" is here used to include both direct competition—those with products and technologies similar to our own—and indirect—those who can meet the same needs, but use different products or technologies to do so. Note that having made a tentative choice of customer target, we are also beginning to define our competitor targets, for by default they will include all those firms seeking to meet the needs of the same customers we have chosen. This will usually be a subset of the total number of customers in the market, however, since not all competitors seek the same customer target.

We should also refine our competitive targets more closely. If we are largest and strongest in the market, it can be argued that we can be less delicate in competitive positioning. Thus, a Coca-Cola may have more leeway in the soft drink market than does Pepsi, 7-Up, Schweppes or RC. For all the other competitors, however, competitor targeting is very important and for the smallest, vital. One useful way to help frame this part of the positioning is to divide competitors into two categories—those with which we would like to compete, and those with which we do not wish to compete. This division should be helpful in devising the core strategy, as well as providing valuable assistance to the salesforce in developing the sales strategy (Chapter 8). In general, we will wish to avoid head-on competition with those stronger than ourselves since we may provoke a strong response, while concentrating our efforts against those who are weaker. Exceptional situations do, of course, occur, but they should be approached with great caution, lest the elephant step on the mouse!

Core Strategy

The final element of the positioning trilogy, the core strategy, describes how we plan to compete for our targeted customers. We must provide a convincing answer to a deceptively simple question: Why should this customer buy from me instead of from my competitor? We must now, therefore, decide which benefit or benefits we are going to focus on providing to our targeted customers. These are several principles to remember when makng this decision, but basically we should be bearing in mind that it will be difficult to develop a very successful strategy unless we are a) focussing on important customer needs and b) attempting to meet them better than competitors. In other words, in designing our core strategy, we are now making our concept of a differential advantage (Chapter 3) operational in a particular product-market area. In addition, wherever possible, we should be seeking to offer benefits that will be difficult for our competitors to imitate, since otherwise we shall be unlikely to gain anything but a temporary advantage, which is less worthwhile.

There are other terms we could have used to describe the idea of the core strategy. The term "key buying incentive" comes close to capturing the concept, while Ted Bates advertising agency's idea of the U.S.P. (the unique selling proposition) is similar, but none captures the key concept as well as core strategy. The reason is not only because these benefits become the key competitive weapon in our positioning that will, therefore, help us capture the customers we seek. They also become the *core* of our strategy in terms of defining what we need in the rest of our marketing mix and supporting functions. Thus it is the benefit or benefits enshrined in our core strategy around which we should organize the copy of our advertising, our selling approach, sales promotion and so on, and, having made that commitment to customers, we must ensure that other functions are committed to delivering those benefits — a subject we explore later in the chapter.

Developing the Positioning Strategy is probably the most laborious and difficult part of product/market strategy development. Although we have described it linearly and sequentially — as written communication forces us to do — it is a complex, creative and highly interactive process, often involving many cut-and-try attempts and simulated testing before we arrive at a satisfactory combination. For example, we may well choose a segment or a competitor target where we know we have a strong advantage, and in this case the core strategy might dictate the choice of customer or competitor targets. More typically, however, we might follow a process such as that de picted in Figure 6-3, beginning with a preliminary choice of customer target and working our way through a process of consistency checks to arrive at a well-integrated positioning.

Supporting Mix and Functional Requirements

We noted in Chapter 3 that many marketing managers have failed at the job of internal proselytization. Because other functions and even general managers often understand so little of the marketing orientation and its implications, it becomes all too easy for the internal task to remain undone. Yet it should be evident, we believe, that no matter how superb a job we may do in analyzing our external environment and developing our positioning, unless we are able to coordinate the actions of others so as to support and actually *deliver* the benefits, our prospects for success are limited indeed. We have divided this part of the product/market strategy into two components, the first dealing with the marketing mix and the second with other functions.

Marketing Mix Requirements

Almost every basic marketing book provides the need to "integrate the marketing mix, but then proceeds to neglect the concept. Indeed, most marketing books (and in some respects this one is no exception) proceed to "disintegrate" it by structuring their whole content around separate discussion of each of the mix elements. It is about the core strategy, however, that the mix must be integrated, and it is perhaps easiest to communicate this idea by example.

Let us suppose that we have chosen "product quality"[2] as the basis of our core strategy, then the rest of our mix must be focussed to support this theme. In Chapter 3 we defined five components of the marketing mix — product, promotion, distribution, service and price. Let us examine the implications of our positioning strategy for each of these. First, if the product is of high quality — say in performance and durability — its appearance and brand name should match these attributes to further reinforce the quality concept. Likewise, if we advertise, the copy should focus on quality, and we should be sure that our choice of media and format do not compromise our positioning. Sales promotional materials, such as brochures and display racks, should likewise be of high quality, while we should ensure to the ex-

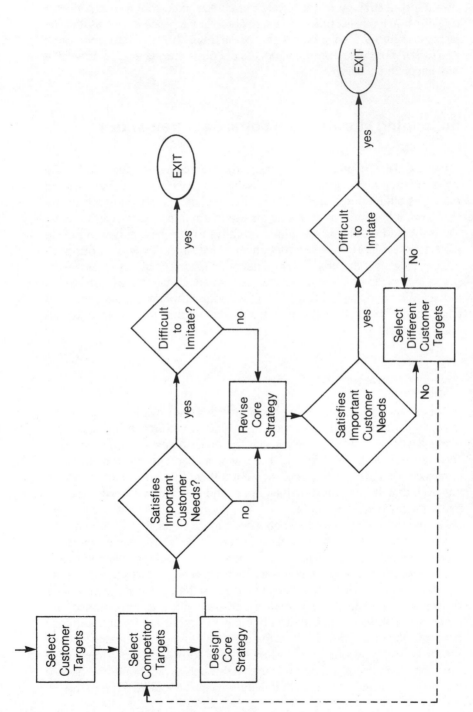

FIGURE 6-3 Developing the Positioning Strategy

tent possible that only "appropriate" (i.e. non-"sensational") publicity be obtained. Selling strategies must also be carefully tailored, while if distribution is involved, both the number and quality of approved distributors should be very carefully scrutinized. If our quality is such that we seek a really exclusive positioning, then we shall use very few distributors of the highest possible caliber. Our service policies must be first-class. If we truly have high quality products, the need for service should be minimal, but when needed, it should be superb. The grudging attitude with which some companies provide service should always be avoided, but in the case of a core strategy of product quality, something special is called for. Finally, we should note that a high product quality leaves us with considerable pricing discretion. Depending on our aggressiveness, we may price anywhere from very high (specialty positioning) to competitive levels (more aggressive) or even lower. We should beware of low prices, however, for at least two reasons. The first is that too low a price will undoubtedly render our quality claims unbelievable to many customers. Secondly, although quality does not necessarily cost money, very high quality almost always does, so that we may incur some cost penalties with this positioning, which would also render price competition foolhardy.

Had we picked some other core strategy, such as low price, rapid delivery or widespread availability, another completely different set of mix implications would have existed. The core strategy is a vital part of the product/market strategy, and provides the parameters within which the advertising, promotion, sales strategies, etc., are developed. Note, however, that many different individuals and even departments may be involved in this process — advertising agencies, the sales department, sales promotion experts, the public relations department, market research suppliers and the like — so that managing this coordination is by no means a simple task.

Supporting Functional Requirements

Finally, of course, we must establish what support we shall require from other departments to implement the proposed strategy. If the requirements cannot be met, we shall be forced back to the drawing board, but unless we clarify what they are we shall be unable to determine whether they can be met and, thus, will be foredoomed to failure.

If we continue with our quality example, there are obvious implications for engineering in product and process design, manufacturing in process control and scheduling, purchasing in procurement policies, finance in providing the necessary funds, technical service in providing backup, customer service in billing, shipping and follow-up, transportation in scheduling and loss/breakage control, etc. A genuine consensus must be built to commit departments and their managers to meeting these requirements, or the strategy is bound to fail.

SUMMARY AND CONCLUSIONS

In this chapter we have reviewed the purposes of the product/market strategy in some detail. As we noted, strategy is often poorly understood, yet it is marketing strategy at the product/market level which is the guts of the firm's marketing effort and also key to its overall success. We then discussed the role of objectives, strategic and operational, building on the strategic concepts developed in Chapters 4 and 5. Clear strategic objectives are prerequisite to sound strategy development yet they are often lacking.

In the remainder of the chapter we developed the elements which should enter into a statement of marketing strategy at the product/market level. As we developed the concept of positioning strategy it became clear that the ability to *deliver* the designed benefits is essential, and we concluded the chapter by returning to the theme of coordination across the marketing mix and supporting functions. In the chapters which follow we shall be examining each mix area in more detail, but we shall be linking the discussion back to Chapter 6, which is crucial to an understanding of the role of the mix in marketing strategy.

REFERENCES AND FOOTNOTES

1. The idea of positioning strategy is more familiar to consumer marketers than to industrial marketers, but exactly the same basic principles apply, including the concept of the three c's.
2. We recognize that there are many aspects to product quality, but for purposes of this example they need not be explored.

7

ADVERTISING AND PROMOTION STRATEGY

In this chapter we shall focus on the strategic decisions involved in advertising and promotion. First, we explore the concept of an integrated communications strategy, with frequent references to the ideas covered in Chapter 6. Then, we take up the issue of advertising strategy, dealing in more depth with such problems as setting advertising objectives and developing copy and media strategy. Finally, we concentrate on the step-child of marketing, sales promotion. It plays an important role in many successful marketing strategies, accounts for very large expenditures, and yet is not always planned as systematically as it should be.

THE COMMUNICATIONS STRATEGY CONCEPT

Coordination and integration, as we have so often stressed in this book, are vital to the successful execution of strategy. Just as this principle applies to the business or marketing strategy, so it applies to the communication elements of the marketing mix (Chapter 3). Too often, however, for reasons reviewed in Chapter 6, companies fail to achieve this integration. Activities of various specialized departments and, sometimes, the role of various outside groups — whether advertising agencies, intermediaries or others — seems to conspire to prevent the achievement of consistent and timely interrelationships among the different elements of the communications mix.

In Chapter 3, we reviewed the basic elements of the promotional mix — advertising, personal selling, publicity and public relations and sales promotion. How can we blend these different elements together in a way which renders their different contributions mutual reinforcing, even synergistic? The only way even to approach this goal is to begin planning the communications strategy as an integrated whole. Unfortunately, as we have just noted, this approach does not sit very comfortably with the way most companies are organized, and, as we noted in the last chapter, it also runs against the somewhat paradoxical practice in marketing of discussing and treating such areas as personal selling, advertising and sales promotion quite separately, even though we preach the need for an integrated marketing mix.

The communications strategy concept necessitates first developing the basic elements of an overall communications plan before refining more specific programs for advertising, sales promotion or even personal selling. Even the overall communications strategy has a more holistic precursor, however — namely the product/market strategy. The sequencing in which key parameters are set would therefore appear as follows:

Elements of the Communications Strategy

The basic parameters of an overall communications strategy are set by the product/market strategy (Chapter 6). These parameters would include the relative importance of communications to the overall strategy and the basis for the message (both of which would be set by the core strategy), the communications targets (from the customer targets), and direction with respect to the kinds of communications objectives which would be set (from the strategic alternatives and the customer targets).

Objectives

Let us examine first the issue of *communications objectives*. Ultimately the overall objective of spending on communications should be to realize larger returns, generally via sales increases which exceed associated cost. More specifically, however, the way in which communications can contribute to this objective is via bringing about change in people's behavior. Thus, the development of communications objectives rests heavily upon the theory of human motivation and behavior change. Our goal, remember, is to communicate to target audiences in such a way that they will be prepared to change their existing or traditional patterns of behavior. How do these changes take place? In many ways — as we now explore. Suppose the product we are advertising is low in cost (less than, say, 25^c U.S., 10p U.K. or Y50) and is quite similar to other products the target market has used — an example would be a new flavor of an existing brand of chewing gum or candy. Then it is quite possible that consumers would make a snap decision to try the product, realizing that the cost of trial is low and they can throw the product away (or pass it on) with little loss if they don't like it. Contrast this example, however, with a decision to buy a car (especially if it is the first car the individual has ever bought) and it would seem self-evident that the decision process is likely to be much more protracted.

One of the most venerable yet convenient ways of viewing this decision process is the so-called "hierarchy of effects" model. First expressed in selling theory in the acronym AIDA — Attention –> Interest –> Desire –> Action,[1] it is more familiar to most people in its more recent advertising formulation: Awareness –> Comprehension –> Attitude –> Intention –> Purchase. The hierarchy of effects model has been much criticized in its simple form since it seems to imply a necessary sequence of steps. As we have shown by example, there is no necessity that this sequence be followed. However, the hierarchy idea does provide a very useful way of summarizing the status of target market at a specific time, and a way to organize our thinking on the setting of communications objectives.

One way to think about communications objectives, therefore, is in terms of the scheme shown in Table 7-1 opposite.

Strategy

Next, we should consider the key elements of the communications strategy itself. Remembering that a strategy guides the allocation of resources in order to achieve objectives, what are the key elements of the

TABLE 7-1 The Hierarchy of Effects and Communications Objectives

Stage	Definitions and Sample Measures
Creating Awareness ⟶	Information that our product exists, is available (often measured by brand recall)
Comprehension ⟶	Information about features of our product (often measured by copy point recall)
Attitude ⟶	Liking for our product (often measured versus competitive products on rating scales)
Intention ⟶	Degree to which customer intends to try/buy our product (often measured by intention surveys)
Purchase ⟶	Actual purchase (can be measured by purchase orders, inventory checks, or, in aggregate, by orders, shipments or sales) Or trial (first purchase)
Repurchase ⟶	Repeat rate or depth of trial, brand loyalty measures, etc.

communications strategy? The answer to this question really lies in answering four other questions which are outlined in Table 7-2 and will now be examined individually.

The *target audience* or audiences must be carefully defined to answer the question "To whom do we communicate." Notice that there may be several key audiences for a given marketing strategy and communications campaign.

Very often we wish to communicate to our distributors and their customers — but since each of these groups purchases our product for very different reasons, the *message* we will use will be very different in each case. The target audience definition should be framed by the customer target(s) specified in the overall product/market strategy — but it will frequently need more refinement and development for purposes of communications planning. The marketing strategist may well overlook some important aspects of the communication targets because of excessive concern with direct customers rather than decision influencers, for example. In fact almost all customer targets have an important vertical dimension as elaborated in the next paragraph.

TABLE 7-2 Elements of the Communications Strategy

Question	Element	Examples
What results do we want?	Objectives	Change attitude Motivate store visits
To whom do we communicate?	Target Audience(s)	Male consumers aged 18-24 Grocery store operators
What do we say?	Message(s)	Story board, print copy
How do we say it?	Tool Allocation	Consumer—advertising sampling Trade—trade advertising, selling
Who says it?	Channel Allocation	Trade—Instore Promotions Advertising—All advertising manufacturer

Take the example of a consumer good sold by the manufacturer to a wholesaler who sells to a retailer and thence to the final consumer. We thus have a chain of customers constituting a channel of distribution for the physical good. As noted in Chapters 3 and 6, manufacturers typically devote some type of marketing research effort to better understanding the segmentation of their consumer markets, often defining consumer market targets more precisely as a result of the study. This might be described as *horizontal* segmentation at the consumer level, and a similar type of segmentation takes place at two other levels when particular wholesalers and retailers are chosen to participate in the channel. There is also, however, a vertical aspect to the choice of market target. By this we refer to the way in which we decide to focus communications effort vertically within the channel. There are two polar approaches to this problem, known as push versus pull strategies, which are depicted in Figure 7-1.

A pull strategy is one in which the manufacturer, say, devotes the vast majority of his communications effort to the final consumer. The underlying rationale is that the resulting buildup of desire for the product at the consumer level will produce a pull-through effect on the rest of the channel, drawing the product into wholesale and retail distribution. This process can be a *resultant*, where the monies are spent generating consumer demand irresistible to intermediaries, or *anticipatory*, where the manufacturer uses his media expenditure plans to convince intermediaries to stock up because of the heavy consumer demand which will result when his advertising breaks.

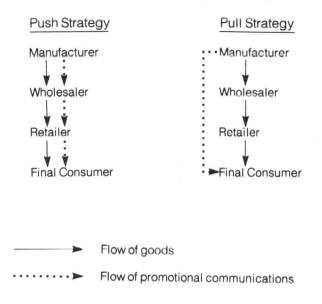

FIGURE 7-1   Push vs. Pull Communications Strategies

The polar alternative is called a push strategy, wherein the manufacturer devotes the bulk of his promotional communications effort to his direct customer, the next customer in the channel. Here the underlying rationale is that we must convince the intermediary that it is in his best interests to apply considerable promotional effort to the product thus generating push down through the channel to the next stage, and so on. Quite clearly, these are polar alternatives, and most strategies are a combination of "push" and "pull," so that defining target audiences and making decisions on the allocation of promotional effort among them is an important and central decision. Unfortunately, as we noted earlier, the different elements of the promotional mix are too rarely the subject of integrated communications plan — but we often see the principle illustrated by the trade-off decisions made by consumer goods brand managers between consumer and trade promotion.

If the chosen strategy approximates a "pull" approach, we typically find that it is much heavier in fixed cost, and involves significant cash outflows. The pre-production necessary to fill the distribution pipeline as well as the plant investment necessary to produce this volume are partly responsible, but the advertising and promotion necessary to generate the "pull" also pose a formidable financial hurdle if pursued on a broad front. One way to deal with this, used in the U.S. market by Japanese and European companies, as well as companies of American nationality, is the so-called regional roll-out which, at the risk of slowing the introductory stage, lowers the financial requirements of pull strategies. In general, however, large companies will find it easier to pursue pull strategies because they can cross-fund from other products in their portfolio. The contrasting push approach is typically heavier in variable costs, since intermediaries are usually provided with their incentive to "push" the product via higher margins. Cash outflows are also more limited since the heavy costs of financing the introductory campaign of advertising and promotion are avoided. For these reasons, smaller competitors are prone to favor push strategies, particularly if they lack other business which might cross-subsidize aggressive entry. Obviously there may also be quite profound differences in the strategic implications of the alternative approaches since, whereas there may be substantial pre-emptive impact from pull strategies, this is much less likely to be the case with a push approach. Canon's bold shift to a pull approach brought them dominance of the U.S. 35mm SLR camera market, while their more push-oriented competitors foundered in Canon's wash.

The message element should present little problem at the level of the communications strategy. The core strategy provides the basis for the message, and as we pointed out in Chapter 6, the core strategy must be developed by segment or target. Different segments may purchase the same product for very different reasons (e.g., motorcycle as transportation vs. leisure good) and different core strategies and messages must be used to communicate with them effectively. Similar reasoning applies to the vertical dimension of the target, since intermediaries buy to resell with the goal of making a profit, and do not have the same interest in functional benefits as do end users or ultimate consumers.

The allocation problems are more complex, but extremely important. With respect to tool allocation, it should be remembered that different communication tools have different capabilities. Personal selling, for example, offers ready two-way communication, and is well suited where a product is complex or requires tailoring to fit the customer's needs well. Almost all advertising is basically one-way, and is typically best suited to communicating reasonably simple, standardized messages to larger audiences which are homogeneous with respect to their needs at fairly low *per capita* cost. Sales promotion techniques, however, are many and varied and can perform a wide range of communication tasks, developed in more detail toward the end of the chapter. A key requirement of developing sound communications strategy, then, revolves around assigning to a particular communications tool the tasks it is well suited to perform in such a way as to produce an integrated whole. Because of the differences in capabilities, it is common to find quite different patterns of use of various communication tools. Some examples of these patterns are shown in Table 7-3, drawn from the U.S. Federal Trade Commission's hearings on advertising.

Just as particular communication tools are well suited to particular tasks,

TABLE 7-3 Role of Personal and Impersonal Communication in Consumer Transactions[1]

	House Sale	Automobile Sale	Appliance Sale	Soap Sale
Role of Middleman	None	Exclusive Retailers Only	Distributor and Non-Exclusive Retailers	Chain Retailers Only
Personal Selling to Consumer	All important	Very important by retailer	Not too important by retailer	Chain Retailer Only
Need for National Advertising	None	Important, but not relative to cost	Somewhat important relative to cost	Very important
Need for Research Feedback	None	Important relative to cost	Somewhat important relative to cost	Very important

so are intermediaries better suited for some aspects of the communications jobs. The push vs. pull alternatives indicate just how much the responsibility for promotional communcation can vary. Consider, for example, the amount of personal selling we can expect from intermediaries. Many distributors are no more than stockists who fill orders, while others very actively sell. In retailing, there is typically a declining amount of personal selling as we move from specialty through department stores to discount stores. On the other hand, discount stores might be the most willing to engage in cooperative advertising or extensive point-of-purchase display and promotion. The best decisions on channel allocation of communications tasks demand an intimate knowledge of particular markets on a case-by-case basis. The important point to bear in mind is that typically we cannot and should not attempt to do everything ourselves, and as we point out in Chapter 9, innovative marketing strategies often revolve around redistribution of tasks among channel members.

THE ADVERTISING STRATEGY

In many respects, the advertising strategy represents a successive refinement of the basic ideas outlined in the marketing and communications strategies. However, as we mentioned earlier, advertising is very often a key element in the product/market strategy, particularly for frequently purchased nondurable consumer goods, and there is therefore an immense amount of effort and thought devoted to it. Although we do not wish to argue against devoting so much effort to something so clearly important, it is often the case that equally important aspects of the marketing strategy receive less effort. Perhaps the powerful role usually played by a specialized (outside) advertising agency involved in the development of the advertising strategy, has something to do with this. Such involvement occurs less often for sales promotion, for example, and is even less usual (except for consulting involvement) on the personal selling side. Be that as it may, there are some key elements which must be attended to in a sound advertising strategy, and these are outlined in Table 7-4.

TABLE 7-4   Elements of the Advertising Strategy

Element	Linkage to Product/Market and Communications Strategies
Objectives	From objectives, tool allocation of communications strategy
Target Audience(s)	From communications strategy
Copy Design - Benefits - Evidence - Context	Message—communications strategy Core strategy—product/market strategy
Media Selection	Target Audience(s) (above)

Objectives for advertising should, of course, devolve directly from the objectives developed in the overall communications strategy, as well as the way in which communication tasks were allocated among various promotional tools. Again, advertising objectives are many and varied, but the adoption of a framework based on some version of the hierarchy of effects-—e.g., Awareness —> Comprehension —> Attitude —> Intention —> Purchase is most useful. Within this framework, many more specific objectives may be designed. During the Federal Trade Commission's hearings on advertising in the early seventies, many examples were provided by advertisers. We list some of these in Table 7-5 below.

To qualify as useful advertising objectives, of course, these general verbal statements would have to be made operational. The Table 7-5 objectives

TABLE 7-5 Examples of Advertising Objectives for a Manufacturer's Product Advertising[2]

To Increase Sales Directly, by:

1. Encouraging potential purchasers to visit dealers or distributors;
2. Announcing special sales, contests, or other promotions;
3. Securing new dealers or distributors;
4. Inducing professional person (*e.g.*, doctor, architect) to recommend a product;
5. Distributing coupons to be redeemed on purchases.

To Create Awareness and Interest in the Company's Products by:

6. Informing potential buyers about product features;
7. Announcing the availability of new products;
8. Demonstrating the benefits of a product's uses;
9. Comparing a product with competing products;
10. Showing how a product should be used;
11. Informing potential buyers about the company's technical skills, product facilities, technical services, etc.
12. Informing purchasers about where products can be obtained;
13. Announcing changes in prices, packages, labels, etc.;
14. Publicizing a new brand name or symbol.

must therefore be stated quantitatively, and within a time frame, although the latter condition is often met by setting objectives for a particular advertising campaign — viz., the objective of the campaign is to raise unaided recall of product X's brand name from 10 to 25%, an example of an awareness objective.

Target audiences, as described earlier, may be multiple. In an industrial context, for example, we may wish to reach a number of different decision-influencers, while in the consumer area the trade — as well as consumers themselves — are often important advertising targets. Again, the overall communications strategy defines overall audiences, and the allocation of tasks to different promotional tools specifies which will be key targets for our advertising. Some further refinement and testing may yet be necessary, but the basic parameters are already determined.

Copy design is an area of much art and some science. Of course, the message we wish to communicate should be embedded in the communications strategy as a result of decisions made in the product/market strategy. The message will normally be focused on key benefits which we wish to communicate, reflecting our differential advantage. To turn this basic statement into effective copy, however, is a daunting and challenging task, where the much-vaunted "creative" aspects of advertising come into play. We happen to believe that substantial creativity is involved in the design of any good strategy, but would be the first to agree that in the design of good advertising copy[3] lies a very high order of creativity.

There is a considerable tradition of research on the design of effective communications. From the early work of Hovland and his group,[4] through more recent efforts, well summarized by McGuire,[5] some generalizations have emerged. There is little evidence, however, that this work has had great influence on the design of advertising,[6] although some ideas are undoubtedly used. Generally, various creative approaches are developed in rough form (for TV advertising as storyboards, for example) and subjected to preliminary evaluation, which may include some testing. The most promising are selected for further development and more extensive testing, which may extend to simulated or "on air" exposure testing, and final choices eventually reached.

What, then, should be the role of the marketing executive in evaluating and managing this aspect of his advertising strategy? There are several key elements in which he must be involved lest the agency stray in a direction which may threaten the coordination of the overall strategy. The first area is that of the primary benefits or claims to be presented. These must be kept on track with the core strategy or much effort will have been wasted. The second area concerns the evidence to be presented to support those claims or benefits. It should be clearly presented and unqualifiedly supportable. Not only can failure in this area prove acutely embarrassing, it may cost millions in lost business and, in many countries, violate the law. Note that we do not wish to imply that advertising agencies have any particular tendency to misrepresent. Rather, the difficulties of presenting certain kinds of evidence may lead to seemingly innocuous but potentially damaging short cuts, and this is an area where, in any case, most agencies are likely to require considerable technical (if not legal) backup from their client.

A final aspect of the copy design process which should be subject to careful overview and involvement is what we call the copy context. Here we mean no more than *how* the benefits are presented. Should we use four-color bleed or black and white? Who should be the product spokesmen? What should be the emotional context — cool, excited, happy, etc.? The context is crucial to the success of the advertisement in communicating what we intend, and must be very carefully developed.

The last element in the advertising strategy is the selection of media. Again, this is a complex and involved subject to which we can give limited attention. The key considerations, however, revolve around the effect that is obtained for a given expenditure. The first criterion must be choice of media to which our target audience is exposed. Beyond this, however, the problem becomes more difficult. First, we must introduce the concept of reach, which is the unduplicated audience of a given vehicle, often expressed as a percent of households or population. Usually more important, however, is the proportion of a vehicle's audience that is in our target audience, sometimes called effective reach.[7]

More complex again, however, is the issue of repetition. For our purposes, we shall define repetition as exposure or noting of the same insertion of an advertising message by the same audience of an advertising vehicle.[8] Frequency refers to the mean number of exposures over the net unduplicated audience for the duration of a campaign.[9] The distinction between the concepts should be clarified by reference to Figure 7-2. Consider an advertising campaign consisting of one advertisement and two insertions. If the audience exposed to the first insertion is 100 persons, shown as A_1, this is also the net unduplicated audience (reach of the first in-

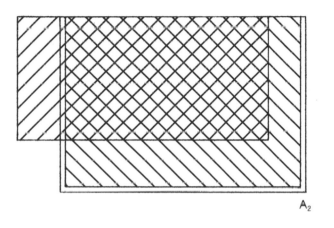

A_2

Key A_1 = 100

A_2 = 110

$A_1 \cap A_2$ = 80

$$A_1 \cup A_2 = A_1 + A_2 - (A_1 \cap A_2) = 130$$

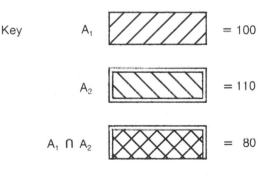

FIGURE 7-2   Repetition and Frequency

sertion). Each was exposed to the ad once. The second time the ad is inserted, however, the number of people exposed is 110, shown as A_2. Of A_2, 80 were also members of A_1 (i.e., were exposed to the first insertion), and 30 were being exposed to the ad for the first tme, since they were not exposed to the first insertion.

The net unduplicated audience is equal to the total of the 20 persons in A_1 who were exposed to the first insertion only, the 80 persons who were exposed to both insertions (written as $A_1 \cap A_2$), and the 30 persons in A_2 who were exposed only to the second insertion. Therefore, the net unduplicated audience (written as $A_1 \cup A_2$) is 130 persons. By our definition, the only persons subject to repetition were the 80 persons who were exposed to both insertions. The frequency, however, is a weighted mean divided by the net unduplicated audience. Each member of the audience is weighted by the number of times he was exposed. Thus,

$$\text{Frequency} = \frac{(30 + 20)1 + (80)2}{130}$$

$$= \frac{210}{130}$$

$$= 1.61$$

Because no two audiences of a given vehicle are identical the frequency will be less than the number of insertions.

Some repetition is generally viewed as desirable. However, the generalizable knowledge about the benefits of repetition is still limited. Ray and Sawyer[10] have summarized evidence, based on laboratory and field studies suggesting that the effect of repetition varied depending upon:

(i) The criterion measure employed.

Recall, brand mention, beliefs, attitudes, purchase intention, and coupon redemptions were all used as measures of effect.

The level, shape, and slope of the repetition ... varied so that the measures ... lower on the response hierarchy (e.g., recall, mention) were affected more than "higher" measures (such as attitude, intention and coupon action). Depending on the measure, the shape of the repetition function was linear, negative exponential or s-shaped. In some cases the functions were flat or even negative.[11]

(ii) Segments.

Brand and product usage were important determinants of the effect of repetition in one study, depending upon whether consumers were users of the test band, the competitive brand, both brands, or neither.

(iii) Product type.

Repetition of ads for nine convenience goods showed a "sharp linear curve" for recall, a gentler curve for intention. In contrast, the recall repetition function for nine shopping goods "flattened after four exposures," while the intention function was almost flat.

Advertisements for well-known brands produced "higher and sharper curves" than did advertisements for less well-known brands, while further differences in repetition were found by ad format, type of illustration, use of color, scheduling, one-sided vs. comparative appeals, and consideration of competitive advertising.

What are the implications of this work for our purposes? While it is clearly wrong to suppose that nothing is known about the effects of repetition, these findings suggest that such effects are highly situation-specific. Sweeping generalizations are therefore suspect, and the issue best approached on a case-by-case basis.

Obviously, however, a given advertising campaign will usually involve the use of a variety of vehicles, if only because the reach of any given vehicle is limited. In such cases the analysis of reach and frequency becomes much more difficult, even though operations research has offered some help.

It should be evident by now that the ability to make media selection decisions optimally is limited to simpler cases. A number of useful computer models have aided decision makes to make "better" media decisions, but the role of judgment is still important. Indeed, in media planning too, creativity and subjective factors are very important. One imaginative agency media man once described his job as finding ways to fill the empty spaces in people's lives with advertising messages. This may be carrying things too far for some, but new media ideas continue to evolve, whether they take the form of sponsored bus stops, ads in paperback books, giveaway records or some other innovation. Certainly the impact created by novel use of media can sometimes compensate for lack of dollars in the advertising budget.

SALES PROMOTION STRATEGY

We have left our discussion of sales promotion to the last part of the chapter for a number of reasons. First, because of the enormous variety of sales promotional tools it is, as we shall see, a subject for a very specific type of planning. Second, although sales promotion is the key element in some communications strategies, for most companies it does not play the central role so often assumed by advertising or personal selling. Third, we believe that the basic principles developed thus far in this chapter will suffice to guide the development of most sales promotion strategies, with some appropriate adjustments which we will now discuss.

Throughout our discussion of communications strategies we have placed great stress on development of objectives. Nowhere is this more important than in the area of sales promotion. Since sales promotional devices and their uses are so varied, the tasks they accomplish are also. For example, consider the use of a cents-off (reduced price) coupon. Included in the package offering cents off on the next unit, it would encourage repeat purchase. If dated, it may encourage consumer inventory-building. If distributed in a magazine, however, it might also induce trial among non-users. We can also include coupons for other products, related or unrelated, of our own manufacture or even for someone else.

In Table 7-6, we have listed some examples of different sales promotion techniques — although it is important to remember that new techniques are being created all the time. How should we make choices among these alternatives? The techniques chosen as well as their mode of application should flow from the direction of the overall product/market strategy, as suggested by Figure 7-3. Sports sponsorship, for example, is often a way to get the name of the company and/or its products quickly and widely disseminated, even though it may have little direct effect on sales. Similarly, inducing trial solely by the use of advertising or personal selling can be very expensive — thus sampling, giving away small sample packs of the product,

TABLE 7-6 Sales Promotion Techniques and Uses

Technique	Possible Use
Sampling	Induce trial (for new product) Induce switch (existing product)
Deals	Increased use Pre-emptive inventory building
Premiums	Trial, repeat, increased use, etc.
Trade Shows	Awareness, interest, attitude, intention, purchase, repurchase, etc.
Sponsorship of Sports	Corporate image and general public relations Induce trial (if sole concession possible)
Point of Purchase Display	Induce trial, increase use, facilitate purchase, increase interest, comprehension
Literature	Interest, comprehension, increased use, etc.
Games	Trial, repeat, increased use, etc.

is often used. Many uses of sales promotion, however, are defensive — used selectively to limit the encroachment of a new brand, for example. In this case, in-pack cents-off coupons might be used to build consumer inventory prior to or during a competitor's introduction. In the case of a product being phased out, or in a category in long-term secular decline, however, it may make sense to cut right back on advertising and focus on a push strategy, with heavy marketing to the trade and use of point of purchase (POP) displays.

The above ideas, then, are not definitive guides to action in every situation, but provide a broad illustration of the right way to approach these decisions. First, we need to assure ourselves that the sales promotion strategy is working in a direction consistent with the overall marketing strategy. Second, we must carefully define the objectives of our sales promotion activity — which should be facilitated by a well-thought-out set of communications objectives and task allocation to tools. The design and distribution of the sales promotional materials is beyond the scope of a general treatise like this, except to caution that most companies use a variety of outside groups and agencies in this part of the communications strategy. In this

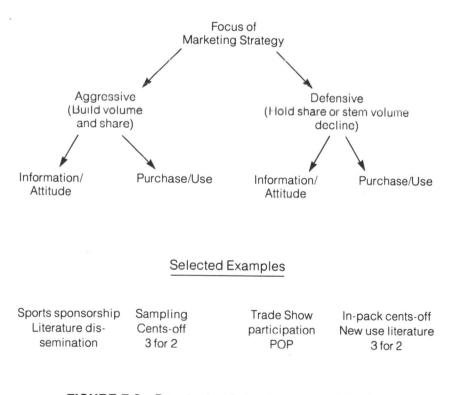

FIGURE 7-3 Developing Sales Promotion Objectives

area, more than any other, there is tremendous variability in quality and some history (at least in the United States) of charlatanism. It behooves the executive to move very very cautiously in this area, since a promotional *faux pas*—such as has occurred with some of the promotional games which came into vogue a few years ago—can be very costly indeed.

SUMMARY AND CONCLUSIONS

There are those who confuse advertising with marketing, believing that marketing begins and ends with its advertising content. Not only is this a dangerous attitude, it is also completely inaccurate for, as we have seen in the chapters we have covered so far, there is much, much more to marketing. Nonetheless, for many goods and services, and most particularly for those marketed to large customer targets via pull strategies, advertising is the key element in the mix. Vast amounts are spent for media coverage and, relatively often very large amounts for advertisement production, also. Yet, although this fact may be recognized, what is less often acknowledged is the fact that, in aggregate, expenditures on two other elements in the promotional mix, personal selling and promotion, are even greater than advertising expenditures. Indeed, in some launches, sampling costs alone may outstrip advertising. What is unfortunate, though, is that even where advertising is well planned, personal selling and sales promotion are often less attended to. The consequence is a very poorly coordinated overall strategy with little chance of success. In this chapter, therefore, we have emphasized heavily the need for an integrated approach to planning the communications strategy. The responsibility for this job lies clearly with the marketing executive—it cannot be fobbed off on the agency, and woe betide the marketing manager who is so derelict in his duty.

REFERENCES AND FOOTNOTES

1. Edward K. Strong, *The Psychology of Selling*, New York: McGraw-Hill, 1925, p. 9.
2. From John A. Howard and James Hulbert, *Advertising and the Public Interest*, Chicago: Crain Communications, 1973, p. 23.
3. Note we are using the word inclusively here, to subsume electronic media.
4. C. I. Hovland, I. L. Janis and H. H. Kelley, *Communication and Persuasion*, New Haven: Yale University Press, 1953.
5. William J. McGuire, "The Nature of Attitudes and Attitude Change," in the *Handbook of Social Psychology*, Eliot Aronson and Gardner Lindzey, eds., Vol. 3, 2nd Ed., Reading, Mass.: Addison-Wesley, pp. 136-314.
6. Howard and Hulbert, *op. cit.* pp. 52-53.
7. Richard E. Stanley, *Promotion*, Prentice-Hall, Englewood Cliffs, N.J.: 1982, p. 233.
8. D. B. Lucas and S. H. Britt, *Measuring Advertising Effectiveness*, New York: McGraw-Hill, 1963, p. 214.
9. *Ibid.*, p. 203.
10. M. S. Ray and A. G. Sawyer, "Behavioral Measurement for Marketing Models: Estimating the Effects of Advertising Repetition for Media Planning," *Management Science*, Vol. 18, No. 4, Part 2 (December 1971), pp. P-73 to P-89.
11. *Ibid.*, p. 9-75.

8

FIELD SALES
STRATEGY

In this chapter, we examine the areas of field sales strategy. Personal selling is not only a key element of the marketing mix (Chapter 3), it is also very often the most critical activity in assuring the implementation of overall strategic plans. The reasons for this may be self-evident in much industrial marketing, where personal selling is so important. However, the importance is no less marked in consumer marketing. Here, it is true, advertising and promotion are often very important — but it is also true that these activities may be quite tightly controlled and coordinated by a marketing group. In achieving and maintaining distribution, setting up and servicing promotional displays and servicing customers, however, the activities of the sales force are central, and it is at this point that marketing becomes crucially dependent upon the ability to act through the sales force to achieve implementation of the marketing strategy.

This key interface between sales and marketing has, in many companies, been poorly managed. Historically, some antipathy was not unusual, for in the U.S. and Europe the growth of marketing departments in the nineteen fifties and sixties frequently meant that the responsibility for a number of activities moved from the sales department to the new marketing department. Further, the marketer's view that sales is only one part of marketing is news to many sales managers — who might never get comfortable with the idea in any case. Whether due to historical rivalry, or more contemporary reasons, however, there is still the danger that sales may plan its activities in one way and marketing in another, producing conflict which may well compromise the firm's success in the marketplace. To help avoid this problem, this chapter will stress the need for very close coordination of sales and marketing strategies. First, then, we consider the major purposes of sales strategy — what it is designed to accomplish. Second, we review the key elements (decisions) which should be part of the sales strategy. Finally, we summarize by comparing the key elements of the sales strategy with the elements of a product/market strategy.

PURPOSE OF SALES STRATEGY

We may define the sales strategy in terms of the purposes it is designed to accomplish. The most important of these, of course, is to allocate the sales resources available in a way which will best accomplish the overall sales objectives. In this respect, then, a sales strategy is comparable to any other strategy, in that it deals with designing *means* to achieve *ends* (objectives). As for other strategies, however, we shall restrict the concept of sales *strategy* to broad or general guides to the allocation of effort. The specific steps we shall specify in the sales *program*, which is generally comprised of the sales action plans of individual sales representatives, supervisors and managers.

In fulfilling the purpose above, however, there are a number of additional *functions* that a sales strategy must also fulfill. These are summarized below.

Implement Product/Market Strategies. As we noted in the introduction to the chapter, personal selling activities are usually among the key elements involved in implementing the product/market strategy. It therefore follows that they *must* be carefully coordinated and integrated with various marketing strategies if the firm is to succeed. The framework we shall present reinforces this integrative role, but it is fair to say that the interface between sales and marketing is a major impediment to successful strategy implementation in many companies.

Specify How to Deal with Customers and Competitors. Obviously customers and competitors are two of the key sets of players in any strategy problem. Indeed, there is no department in the firm that lives closer to both customers and competitors than the salesforce — and allocation of effort among alternative customer and competitive targets is a key decision problem for the sales manager and his people. A sales strategy should help deal with this problem by indicating what will be the best allocation of effort. In doing so, the sales strategy will usually become much more specific than marketing strategy, which deals with these issues — but only in generic terms.

Specify How the Salesforce Will Spend Its Time. It is important to recognize that the primary purpose of a sales strategy is to allocate sales effort. However, since from moment to moment, at least (if not from week to week), the sales manager cannot control the level of effort *per se*, we must deal with *time* instead. Note that we are, at best, allocating an *input* to the sales process. What results (*output*) — whether a sale, a decision to examine or test our product or service, or merely more favorable attitudes — depends upon not just the sales effort, but everything else incorporated in our offer and our business and marketing strategies.

Before moving on to the content of a field sales strategy, we should also point out a deliberate limitation we shall impose on our discussion. Quite clearly, sales persons perform (or should perform) a variety of tasks as part of their job. Activities which often form part of the sales job include:

- Selling
- Travelling
- Intelligence-gathering
- Checking inventory
- Customer service
- Training and education
- Collections
- Participating in meetings
- Communicating
- Record-keeping
- Planning
- Merchandising
- Credit checking

and others. The importance of each of these activities varies greatly, depending on the firm, the way it is organized and so on. An important part of the sales manager's job involves deciding how their salesforce should divide its time among these activities. In considering sales strategy, however, we focus primarily upon the use of *selling* time, although we shall recognize that the issue of how much time should be spent on selling, as opposed to other activities, must be resolved by sales management.

CONTENT OF A SALES STRATEGY

Following our ends-mean definition, we shall first discuss objectives, then the specific resource allocation decisions that must be made in the sales strategy.

Sales Objectives

In discussing sales objectives, we distinguish two types: business objectives and action objectives. The former consist of some financial or market measures of business performance — e.g., profits, sales volume, profitability, costs, etc., whereas the latter are not directly related to such measures. Action objectives might include having all of the salesforce receive specialist product training by June 30, 198X, having 2,000 in-store promotional displays set up by March 31, 198Y, and achieving an average 90% topbox score on customer service in the final quarter of 198Z. Note that action objectives are often extremely important, even though their link to performance may be indirect.

Business Objectives

One of the key goals in developing business objectives for the salesforce should be to ensure their consistency with the objectives developed in the business and product/market strategies. This is less difficult for a specialized salesforce, but can be a major problem when utilizing general or pooled salesforces. Consider a situation where six products, each of which has a product manager, must be sold through the same general or "pooled" salesforce. If the company plans by product (which is very common), each of these products will have its own set of market and financial objectives. As we noted in Chapters 5 and 6, some of these might be growth objectives, others profitability or cash flow maintenance, and yet others may involve planning for rapid decreases in sales, share and profits as a product is phased out or quickly harvested. To incorporate these differences in product marketing objectives into business objectives for the salesforce is a complex task of translation, since salesforces are usually organized geographically. It must take place, however, to achieve the consistency which will permit implementation of the overall marketing strategy.

The way in which marketing objectives are translated into sales objectives is also crucial. Since territories (or customer lists) vary in their market and sales potentials and workload characteristics, and salespeople similarly vary in their capability and motivation, the conversion of general product sales objectives into specific region, area, territory objectives must be suitably individuated. A blanket, across-the-board transmutation of general goals into subgoals is certain to be suboptimal. This process of breaking down overall objectives into subgoals for specific sales control units, then, is a critical activity, frequently involving much discussion and negotiation, and is best performed when accompanied by ample "bottom-up" information on territory sales potentials, customer and competitive characteristics and qualities of salespeople and their managers.

For most organizations, business objectives for the salesforce are stated in volume measures of some type, often because companies are reluctant to reveal margin information to their salespeople. Companies expressing concern about profitability, or excessive volume orientation among their salesforces might do well to consider more fully the implications of this practice, but we shall focus on sales volume objectives since they are the most commonly used. In today's world, however, volume objectives should, we believe be stated in several ways, *viz.*:

- Sales units   __ units are typically the key concern of manufacturing/operations and purchasing, and this measure is therefore key for them

- Sales dollars   (current or nominal)
  — The most "typical" measure, which incorporates expectations about selling prices, and is used by the traditional, historically based accounting system for both budgeting and record keeping

- Sales dollars   (real or deflated)
  — a vital measure in inflation-riddled economic environment.

Examples of different kinds of volume objectives are shown in Table 8-1. In the context of action planning for individual salespeople or supervisors, however, these objectives would be broken down yet further, to the level of individual territories, customer classes within territories or — for companies where a relatively small number of large customers are very important — individual key accounts.

TABLE 8-1   Examples of Salesforce Business Objectives

Units	Sales objectives for Region A in fiscal 198X are to sell 92,000 lbs. of Product A and 18,000 lbs. of Product B
Current Dollars	Sales objectives for Region B in fiscal 198X are to sell $1,365,000 (198X Dollars) of Product A and $323,000 +198X Dollars) of Product B
Real Dollars	Sales objectives for Region C in fiscal 198X are to sell $1,130,000 (Constant 1978 Dollars) of Product A and $231,000 (Constant 1978 Dollars) of Product B.

Action Objectives

As for business objectives, action objectives should be stated in terms which are specific, results-oriented, and which state a time frame. The multiplicity of possible action objectives for the salesforce means that we can only show a few representative samples. Many action objectives, however, will be related to kinds of activities discussed below. Thus, typical action objectives might be of the type shown in Table 8-2.

TABLE 8-2   Examples of Salesforce Action Objectives

Training	All salespeople to have completed selling skills refresher course by June 23, 198X.
Planning	All salesperson action plans to be completed and accepted by December 5, 198X.
Inventory Checking	Checks of distributor inventories to be completed by October 1, 198X.
Call Reports	Call reports to be telephoned in to local office within 24 hours of call completion.

The Table 8-2 examples should indicate that desirable characteristics of action objectives include brevity, specificity, clarity and time goals. They often relate to completion of activities which are means to the end of accomplishing the salesforce business objectives.

Sales Focus

Having established objectives, the selling effort must be allocated in a way which will enable the attainment of the sales objectives. There are four specific areas in which the strategy should specify a focus: activities, customers, product line and new business. Each will now be examined.

Activity Focus

The purpose of the activity focus statement is to provide guidance by which to allocate the efforts of the field salesforce among different kinds of activities. Typically, in fairly mature markets, the overall balance of activities is likely to vary little from planning period to planning period. In fast-changing markets however, whether growing or declining, more rapid changes in activity focus are likely to take place.

In entering new markets, for example, the salesforce would normally be expected to spend greater proportions of its time on such activities as gathering competitive intelligence, estimating customers' volume requirements and desired product mix, training intermediaries and retailers and making introductory calls. Later in the development of the market, the activity mix will likely focus on more selling and promotion. In market decline for a product, the focus of the activities of the salesforce is likely to be on consolidation of distribution, facilitating liquidation, disposal or reassignment of inventory, making collections and so on.

Although the examples just discussed are quite detailed, more general categories may suffice. The key point is to recognize that the sales manager must develop guidelines for how the salesforce is to spend its time which are consistent with the sales objectives which have been established. If we take as an example general salesforce activity categories of selling, serving, travelling and administration, the activity focus should set an allocation goal, which might be (example only):

Activity	Max or Min	% of Total Time Available
Selling	Minimum	25%
Travelling	Maximum	30%
Servicing	Minimum	30%
Admininstration	Maximum	10%
(Miscellaneous)	—	5%
		100%

Note that these guidelines would be established as general, overall targets for the salesforce as a whole. Individual territories and salespeople might vary considerably from this average due to differences in sales potentials, workloads, etc. Note also that the schedule does not attempt to account for all time (or all activities), but is simply a means of attempting to establish some activity priorities.

Customer Focus

This is a second major focus that should be established by a field sales strategy. In other words, the strategy should specify the overall goals for allocation of time among different types of customers. This involves establishing norms for call time and call frequency for different customers or customer types. Again, when numbers of customers are small (key accounts), these norms may be set for individual customers. More typically, however, they will be established by type or class of customer. The call norms will ideally be based on a good appraisal of sales potential and ex pected response to given calling patterns, and operations research now offers considerable help to the manager in this area.[1]

A sample customer focus schedule might, then, look as follows:

Customer Type	Call Time	Call Frequency
A	1 hour	2/month
B	½ hour	1/month
C	20 minutes	1/quarter
D	10 minutes	when possible

It should be emphasized, however, that again these are not rigid standards, but are overall guides which the sales manager wishes to be observed in allocating effort. From these standards, however, we can manage the overall customer focus if we know numbers of customers in each class.

Product Line Focus

In many companies, a considerable amount of planning effort is focussed around products. Engineers and designers, manufacturing managers and — in many companies — marketing managers (called product managers) are organized and work on this basis. As a result of a great deal of thought and effort, then, products are developed and launched. Different kinds of objectives may be developed for different products (as discussed in Chapter 6) and, as we noted at the beginning of this chapter, these should be translated into a consistent set of sales objectives. To achieve these differing objectives, however, also means that the different products should receive an appropriate amount and direction of selling effort. This is the overall purpose of the product line focus statement in the sales strategy. It is a crucial step in the implementation of overall business and marketing strategies, since to achieve these objectives it is essential to ensure consistent effort allocation. Yet, it is a step often omitted in companies' planning.

The product line focus statement, then, specifies how selling time will be allocated among the different products in the line. The focus can be established with differing degrees of sophistication. In its most elementary form, it would attempt to deal only with product mentions during calls.

Much better, however, is to establish time goals, which is feasible when selling relatively few products or product groups, but would become infeasible for all but a few products where a very broad line is involved. As mentioned earlier, call times should be related to product marketing and sales objectives, which may mean barely mentioning mature products, and spending the majority of call time on newer products.

The field sales strategy, then, will attempt to establish an overall product line focus for the salesforce as a whole, and a sample statement might read as follows:

Selling Time	Product Type
16000 hours	Product A
6000 hours	Product B
4000 hours	Product C

New Business Focus

A final but vital sales focus is the new business focus. Most salesforces (although not all) prefer to spend their time with the familiar — whether customers, applications or products. Yet existing customers, products and applications represent the *today* of the business, much of its *future* may depend on the new. It is essential, therefore, that the field sales strategy attempt to ensure that sufficient time is devoted to meeting new business objectives, and this is the purpose of the new business focus statement.

The new business focus means establishing norms for call time with respect to three important aspects of new business activity:

- New customers (prospecting)
- New products (see product line focus)
- New applications

Note that new products should already have been covered in the product line focus, so that for this aspect, the new business focus is merely a crosscheck.

For fairly mature markets and products, the new business emphasis is likely to be limited, and the new business focus relatively simple to establish. For newer, growth businesses, however, the new business focus is paramount, and establishing priorities is likely to be more difficult and demanding. Theoretically, of course, there are a large number of alternative effort allocations, and a chart such as Figure 8-1 may be helpful to the manager in reviewing the options.

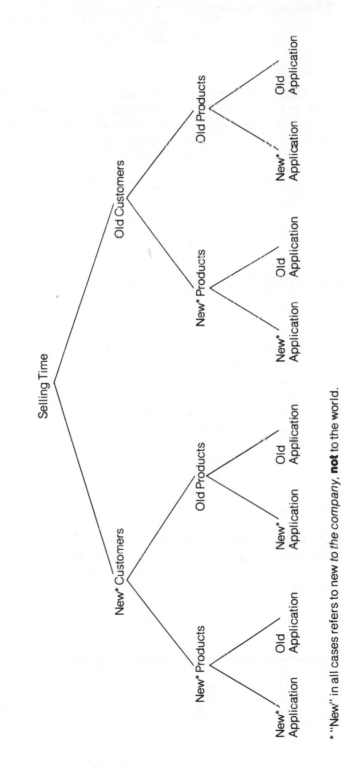

* "New" in all cases refers to new *to the company,* **not** to the world.

FIGURE 8-1 Choosing a New Business Focus

Sales Approach

The sales approach provides the basis for *what* will be communicated to customers, and the goal in developing the sales approach is to select the right things to be communicated, and to communicate them in the right way. The two major constituents of the sales approach are:

- The choice and substantiation of the key benefits which we will use to motivate customers to buy from us

- Design of the process for communicating those benefits to customers

We will now examine each of these components in more detail.

Key Benefits

In Chapter 3 we defined a differential advantage, and in Chapter 6 we pursued this idea further in refining the core strategy statement. In the sales approach, the core strategy is refined still further to tailor the approach to specific competitor targets. Table 8-3 helps to explain the concept.

In Table 8-3, we focus on an individual customer, whose needs we have identified and prioritized, as shown in the two left-hand columns. We assume that the customer is actively considering three alternative sources or suppliers to meet these needs, and we have identified these suppliers as X, Y, and Z. We now examine the problems faced by each supplier, in terms of how to develop a sales approach.

Consider first, competitor X. X is the only company in the "evoked set"[2] of alternatives which has a differential advantage, as defined in Chapter 3. X offers benefit B, second-ranked by the customer, and it is the only one of the three suppliers which can satisfy this particular customer need. A sales approach for this particular customer, then, might stress that X is the only supplier offering B. This approach could also be elaborated to stress that X is the only competitor offering A, B and C, and/or that it offers the best performance with respect to B and C. For competitor Y, a logical sales approach would be to focus on the fact that it offers the best performance on A. Competitor Z's position is relatively weak, and its most feasible approach might be to stress that it offers the best D, and is the only supplier to offer A, C and D.

Table 8-3 also raises some questions, and suggests directions for both

TABLE 8-3 Developing Sales Approaches

Customer Wants			Competitors' Offers						
			X		Y		Z		
Benefit	Ranking	Benefits	Competitive Ranking	Benefits	Competitive Ranking	Benefits	Competitive Ranking		
A	1	A	2	A	1	A	3		
B	2	B	1						
C	3	C	1			C	2		
D	4			D	2	D	1		

market research and product/offer development and modification. First, notice that no competitor of the three offers all benefits sought by the customer — *viz.* A, B, C, and D — and thus all suppliers are vulnerable to a new entrant with a better-matched offer. If we were to ask for which competitor we would prefer to work as a salesperson, competitor Z would not be highly ranked, illustrating how key the marketing strategy is in providing "ammunition" with which the salesforce can perform its assigned job. Note also, however, that the salesforce may well be targeting the wrong customer — *i.e.*, a different customer than marketing designed the offer for, producing a poor match between an offer and this customer's needs.

In terms of marketing research, a number of questions are raised. If this customer's volume requirements are large, or if there are many customers with similar needs, it might pay any of the competitors to develop an offer better matched to customer needs. In addition, ranking of benefits is a rather crude measure. More sophisticated research might enable us to establish the relative importance of different benefits more precisely, and to establish whether or not particular benefits are absolutely necessary or might be relinquished for superior performance on others.

A major advantage of the type of analysis performed in Table 8-3, however, is the sharpening of competitive focus which results. We may now develop a sales approach which is focussed against a specific competitor. In other words, we could be segmenting the customer base by competitive target, as illustrated in the following schedule, which assumes that we are competitor X.

	Competitor	
	<u>Y</u>	<u>Z</u>
Sales <u>Approach</u>	Offer B and C (Y doesn't) with good A	Offer B (Z doesn't) and better A and C

Even so, however, we should note that development of the sales approach is not cut and dried. If D is a low ranked but essential benefit, Y will be in trouble. Similarly, how to deal with Table 8-3 differences is not clear. Should X attempt to depreciate the customers' ratings of A (on which it is second-ranked) or D (which it does not possess)? The marketing concept suggests that this would be less effective than augmenting levels of A and adding D — but clearly there are cost issues involved in such precise segmentation. Finally, there are dangers involved in stressing too many benefits. A large volume of research suggests that human information-processing and decision-making is typically based on relatively few criteria,[3] and incorporating too many benefits in a sales approach may result in confusing the customer, or creating a credibility gap.

Communicating Benefits to Customers

While most sales managers might agree that establishing key benefits to be communicated is a desirable and necessary task, many shrink at the notion of attempting to design the process by which these benefits will be communicated. We should remember, however, that the bulk of sales training expenditures are allocated to improving the communications effectiveness of salespeople, so that this is a perfectly legitimate area in which sales management can attempt to exert some direction. Thus, although complete standardization of process may be an undesirable goal, there are certain key elements of the process where sales management should offer guidance. Briefly, these could include:

- Establishing call objectives: What should the salesperson be attempting to achieve with individual customers at different stages of the buying process?

- Designing need elicitation procedures: What are the key questions the salesperson should ask to establish customer needs and benefits sought?

- Handling objections: What are common objections that might be anticipated and how should the salesperson deal with them?

- Setting "tone" of sales interview: How strident or aggressive should the salesperson be? What time perspective should he/she be working with?

Obviously, to provide guidance in these areas demands not only sensitivity (particularly where more experienced salespeople are involved) but also a sophisticated understanding of the customer buying process. Yet, one good definition of selling is a system designed to facilitate the customers' buying process — and the areas discussed above are certainly central to such a goal.

Implementation Requirements

The final content area of a field sales strategy is to plan for implementation. Three specific requirements must be met to ensure that successful implementation is possible, and each will now be reviewed.

Sales Support Requirements

The successful implementation of any field sales strategy typically depends upon the programming of a myriad of other supporting activities, primarily but not exclusively falling under the general heading of sales promotion. The field sales strategy should specify the necessary support requirements and establish the general means and schedules for their accomplishment. Typical requirements which must be scheduled might be:

- Design, printing and distribution of sales literature
- Reseller training sessions or meeting
- Trade show participation
- Product knowledge training
- Advertising coordination
- Selling skills training.

These requirements would typically be developed by product or product group, then integrated into a support program for the salesforce as a whole.

System Consistency Check

To ensure the maximum likelihood of successful implementation, the field sales strategy should be reviewed to check its consistency with the existing *modus operandi*. Three general elements are key: organization, systems, and people.

Although it may appear obvious, it is important to check that the existing organization structure is consistent with implementation. Are sufficient salespeople available? Do we have adequate levels of supervision? Is the geographic or market allocation of the salesforce consistent with the strategy we are undertaking? Do we have adequate product, technical and market expertise in the existing salesforce organization?

A second key area for a consistency check is systems. One crucial aspect is the sales information and control system. Do we collect appropriate information, in a timely manner, which will enable monitoring implementation of the strategy? Another key element for review is the compensation system — will it facilitate or hinder implementing the chosen strategy. In some companies, differentiated product objectives are developed in the business or marketing strategies, but some kind of blanket salesforce incentive compensation system remains which hinders and sometimes even prevents achievement of those objectives. Compensation consultants are now advocating more complex incentive schemes which more closely link compensation to strategic objectives. Although undue complexity should be avoided in any compensation system, at a minimum the sales manager should be assured that no overt conflict exists between the sales objectives and the compensation system.

Finally, in any endeavor of this type, the people and people climate are crucial. Gaining the necessary support from the field salesforce is much easier if the strategy is consistent with their skills and attitudes, as well as acceptable within the company's political and cultural structure. Certainly, the manager who neglects his internal "market" does so at his peril.

Strategy Incentives

Regardless of the overall compensation system, sales managers should review whether or not additional incentives are desirable in order to get this particular field sales strategy implemented. In the short term, the overall compensation system is not easily changed. Yet sometimes it offers insufficient incentive to provide reasonable assurance that a particular strategy can be implemented. However, it is usually possible for the field sales manager to design and budget additional incentives which might be used, and they could include special bonuses, prizes, evaluation points, "stamp" schemes, training awards and so on. The main purpose is to provide the necessary incentive boost to achieve successful implementation.

SALES AND MARKETING STRATEGY: THE KEY INTERFACE

The foregoing should have made clear the fact that there should exist an intimate and very direct relationship between the sales and marketing strategies. As we noted at the beginning of the chapter, the failure to ensure this close parallel is an unfortunate failing in too many organizations. We shall now summarize the relationships that we have developed in this chapter.

The strategic and operational objectives developed in marketing strategy should be directly reflected in the field salesforce objectives. This correspondence should be most direct for the salesforce business objectives, which should not be exclusively concerned with volume increase, but must reflect the differentiated marketing objectives for the various product/markets in which the salesforce will operate.

The choice of strategic alternatives (Chapter 6) should be related to the sales focus. In new market development, for example, the salesforce activity focus will be quite different from that in more mature markets, as will their new business focus. Likewise, the positioning decisions involved in selecting customer target, competitive target and core strategy will be reflected in both the customer focus and the sales approach, although the latter two are typically developed in much more detail. Product line focus is also a key interrelationship for multiproduct salesforces, since it is here that the crucial decisions are made in balancing off selling efforts for different products. In U.S. companies, the various product managers often become involved in quite protracted tugs of war over this issue, and the conflicts which must be resolved are seldom simple.

Finally, the supporting mix and functional requirements which are incorporated in product/market strategies indicate important relationships to the sales strategy. From the product/market strategy perspective, of course, the sales strategy forms part of the supporting mix, and the product/market strategy should specify the general parameters within which the sales strategy is developed. Implementation requirements in the sales strategy develop and analyze the necessary support activities and systems in greater detail, and in a manner more focussed on the specifics of the sales strategy.

In general, then, there are a number of important interrelationships between sales and marketing strategies, but they may also be contrasted. Whereas the marketing strategy (for product or market) is fairly broad, dealing with rather sweeping and even general allocation decisions, the sales strategy (for product and market) is much more focussed, and more specific. At this level, the sales strategy represents a further focussing and refinement of the marketing strategy, to which it is very closely linked. Ultimately, however, a field sales strategy must be integrated across products and markets, which broadens its domain considerably.

If the reader finds the above logic reasonable, then it might seem paradoxical that coordination problems often arise at the marketing/sales interface. Some have argued that achieving higher levels of coordination and cooperation have been hallmarks of Japanese corporate success, and the "ringi" system may ameliorate the problems in some Japanese firms. In the U.S. and Europe, however, close coordination between sales and marketing is not always achieved. As we noted earlier, historical antipathy is partly to blame, as are (sometimes) poor interpersonal skills, or organizational snafus. In too many companies, however, the planning system itself is to blame. To enable sales objectives and strategies to be developed in the manner we have discussed means that marketing plans must be finished or at least outlined *first*, before sales strategy is developed. Thus, while the formal, written marketing plan need not be completed, sales managers need an outline covering the key Chapter 6 elements before they can develop appropriate sales strategies. In too many companies, the order is inverted, with sales planning completed first (a seeming impossibility!) while in others marketing is so delayed in its planning that it just meets end-of-period deadlines and sales planning is, of necessity, catch-as-catch-can. To reiterate, to develop good sales strategies demands prior outlines (at a minimum) of marketing strategy, and any planning system otherwise sequenced needs modification.

Finally, it is also important to recognize that where a general sales force is employed to sell a range of product groups — as is usually the case — the field sales strategy and the activities of the field salesforce play an essential integrating role. To perform this role well requires careful coordination among product/market managers and sales managers and their respective plans. The coordination problems so often observed, then, have their root not just in bugs in the planning system itself, but also in poor conflict-resolution skills of managers. When the conflict revolves around the allocation of scarce sales resources, it is extremely important that consensus be achieved harmoniously, for the salesforce morale implications of political infighting and internecine conflict can be disastrous.

SUMMARY AND CONCLUSIONS

This chapter has described in some detail the key elements in a field sales strategy. As we observed, successful implementation of such a strategy demands detailed planning and programming beyond that described herein, and much of this should take place in the context of individual salespeople's sales action plans. There are several key concepts which should be emphasized, however.

First, a primary requirement of any sales strategy is that it be designed in such a way as to ensure successful implementation of the overall business and product/market strategies. Close coordination in planning is essential if this requirement is to be met.

Second, the purpose of the field sales strategy is to allocate selling effort — which translates into selling time. The key factors in the allocation process are activities, customers, products and new business. Each of these factors must be carefully evaluated, and guidelines for effort allocation with respect to each should be established. In the absence of such guides, each salesperson and sales manager will be making his/her own decisions independently, and the prospects of successfully implementing overarching strategies are zero.

Third, the sales manager should devote considerable effort to the issue of approaching the customer. What benefits will be stressed and how they will be communicated to the target customer are key questions. The fact that the customer is likely to be actively thinking about buying from a number of other suppliers should not only be considered, but should be actively incorporated in the sales approach.

Finally, the wise sales manager will always review the requirements for implementation. Such problems as poor support; insufficient manpower; compensation, evaluation or promotion systems out of kilter with overall objectives; personal conflicts or lack of sufficient incentive frequently dog the implementation of strategies, and only careful checking can forestall glitches which may turn into disasters.

Naturally, even well-developed sales strategies do not guarantee successful strategy implementation. Operations may be weak, conditions may radically change, or other mix strategies may be the source of the difficulty. However, for many companies, better developed sales strategies could quickly and significantly improve their prospects for successful performance.

REFERENCES AND FOOTNOTES

1. See, for example, Leonard M. Lodish, "CALLPLAN: An Interactive Salesman's Call Planning System," *Management Science*, Vol. 18, No. 4, Part II, December 1971b, pp. 25-40.

2. John A. Howard and Jagdish Sheth, *The Theory of Buyer Behavior*, New York: Wiley, 1969, p. 26.

3. See, for example, George A. Miller, "The Magical Number Seven, Plus or Minus Two," *Psychological Review*, Vol. 63, March 1956, pp. 81-97 and James Hulbert, "Information Processing Capacity and Attitude Measurement," *Journal of Marketing Research*, Vol. 12, February 1975, pp. 104-106.

9

DEVELOPING DISTRIBUTION STRATEGY

The attitude of many manufacturers toward their distributors is lukewarm at best. The ability to reach final customers via mass (and, increasingly, other types of) media has weakened relationships in many channels as manufacturers yield to the temptation to establish and strengthen their direct rather than indirect relationships with final customers. Yet, the development of effective, coordinated and cooperative relationships with distributors is still essential for success in many markets.

Changing technologies, competitive strategies, regulations and customer needs all create pressures on existing distribution systems, causing some channel members to fail while others adapt readily and easily to change. Innovation in distribution has been an important element in improving marketing productivity, yet as these innovations occur, they can bring about cataclysmic change in an industry.

In this chapter, we shall commence by addressing some very basic principles involved in developing sound distribution strategy. Some characteristic misconceptions arise in different types of industries, and it is important to resolve these points of possible confusion before proceeding further. Next we examine the major issues which must be resolved in developing distribution objectives and strategy. We conclude by outlining the key elements which should enter into a well-designed distribution strategy.

KEY PRINCIPLES OF DISTRIBUTION PLANNING

The key principles involved in developing distribution strategy may be summarized as follows:

- Definition and measurement of market;
- Definition and targeting of customers;
- Division of tasks;
- Definition and implementation of standards.

These principles are often ignored to the peril of the company involved.

Distribution planning involves the design, development and management of the intermediary agencies and activities involved in ensuring the satisfaction of our final customer, be it consumer, firm or government. Note that this is a broad view, involving many possible flows and channels, and not restricted to purchase of goods, but involving such elements as delivery of postpurchase service and the like.[1] Common misconceptions arise from just these points, since some are inclined to conceive of distribution in solely physical terms, or to conclude that the distribution job ends at the next channel member. It is also important to notice that although a manufacturer (for example) may have little choice over the channels he uses to reach his market, there is still a lot to be done in designing the distribution strategy and program — choice of intermediaries is only part of the job. Having covered these basic points, let us now turn to the key principles we have just introduced.

Definition and Measurement of Market

It is often said of decisions about channels — and particularly channel members — that they are crucial to the firm because they tend to involve it in long-term enduring relationships with others. It is also true, however, that these relationships do not (or should not) endure forever. Markets change and purchasing patterns change, and so ultimately — of necessity or by choice — must modes of distribution. In some instances, the ability to foster and/or anticipate the change in consumption and/or purchase patterns has wrought revolutionary change in an industry. Hanes L'Eggs™ pantyhose, for example, became the dominant U.S. brand not only because of an eye-catching, beautifully packaged, quality product — but also because it was the first such brand to focus its distribution efforts on supermarkets and drugstores, the "convenience" outlets of modern-day America.

It is in such changes that we see illustrated the importance of the first principle of appropriate definition and measurement of markets. The most important "customers" in any market are those who ultimately consume. For this purpose, then, only the government and the final consumer are really important — for even a user of industrial supplies must have ultimate markets for his products, or his needs for consumable supplies soon disappear. It follows, therefore, that for most companies (the major exception being retailers), the most important customer is not the next customer in the channel — the immediate or proximal customer — but one further down the channel — the proximal customer's customer or even his customer. Note what a difficult and obtuse point this is to communicate with many people — for it says that our most important customer is not the one with whom we deal every day, nor those who give us the money for our goods and services, but someone whom we may never meet nor do business with directly. Of course, some manufacturers understand this point very well. Many large consumer goods companies which spend heavily on advertising and promotion to the ultimate consumer recognize full well that while their trade relations are important, their eventual success is determined by — and impossible without — those customers. Similarly, many sophisticated industrial companies understand this point also. A supplier to the Detroit automobile industry has certainly become aware of the fact that if consumers stop buying Detroit's cars, Detroit will not long continue buying his components — in other words, his demand is a derived demand.

Yet, in many companies, although this point may be understood, it is either forgotten, or we fail to develop and act upon its implications. Here, then, is the key issue for our principle of market definition and measurement, for too many companies make the mistake of conceiving, defining and measuring their markets in terms of the next members of their existing channels of distribution. As changes take place in the purchasing and/or consumption patterns of those who were the customers of those channel members, the ability of our supplying firm to detect and understand them is dependent upon the market information skills of its proximal customers. Very often, then, we may become the unwitting victims of our proximal customers' marketing incompetence.

If good strategic planning commences with a broad view of markets, then good distribution strategy and planning begins with a *deep* view of markets. It is essential to understand the firm's market in depth, to the point of the ultimate "using up" of the good or service (or that good or service in which ours has been incorporated) if we are to come to grips with the dynamics of competitive market places. This often means a willingness to spend some money on primary market research with ultimate customers. Certainly if our market information is limited to that supplied by proximal customers and/or trade associations and government, there is strong reason to be worried about the firm's long-term prospects.

To summarize, the markets wherever possible should be initially framed and defined in terms of the customers who "use up" the good or service, whether it is military armaments, health insurance or bubble gum. Tracking research should focus on changes in usage or purchase patterns. Data gathering cannot be limited to existing intermediaries and/or proximal customers, but must admit the likelihood of new forms of distribution evolving in importance. Finally, although some distribution changes evolve quite slowly, other take place with quite a degree of rapidity, so that quinquennial surveys of distributors are hardly likely to fill the bill!

Definition and Targeting of Customers

This principle is, of course, closely linked to the issue of market definition, and was already introduced from one perspective in Chapters 4 and 5 and developed further in Chapters 6, 7, and 8. If the market in which the firm's product or service is ultimately consumed is served by one or more intermediary levels in a channel, then given the resource constraints under which everyone works, we are faced with some decisions over priorities among the customers at different levels in the channel. In other words, while recognizing that the "ultimate" consumer in the channel is the key to continuance of the market, we may choose to focus different aspects of our total marketing effort at different levels in the channel, and we must also make decisions abut the proportions of our total effort to be aimed at those different levels.

In its most extreme form, this issue resolves into polar promotional strategies of "push" vs. "pull" (Chapter 8), but in the real world the issues are more complex. As we noted in Chapter 3, great marketing success with, say, the ultimate consumer may lead the firm to be neglectful of its trade contacts, thus creating competitive vulnerability to a good trade-based strategy — or vice versa. Thus, distribution planning raises in full extent the issues discussed in Chapter 3, *viz.*, what constitutes a customer. Choosing the degree of emphasis and type of effort placed at each level in the channel is a complex issue involving competitive positioning and a variety of other strategic considerations — but it is an issue demanding very thorough understanding of channel relationships and interrelationships before it may be satisfactorily resolved.

Finally, it is important that we understand that it is the benefits sought by our various customers that should exert the primary influence on the distribution strategy we develop, *not* the type of product or service we are involved in distributing.

Division of Tasks

This principle is central to understanding the economic role of intermediary activity. Consider the kinds of functions performed by intermediaries[2] which might include:

Promotion	Distribution	Services
Advertising	Bulk-breaking	Product Service
Personal Selling	Stocking	Management Services
Sales Promotion	Dispersing	Consulting Services
Publicity	Quality sorting	Additional Guarantee/
	Delivery	Warranty
		Insurance

Financial	Additional Processing
Trade Finance	Fitting and Sizing
Risk-taking	Shaping
Long-term finance	Finishing
Collection	

Clearly, there is a great variety of tasks to be performed in any channel, and central to the development of a sound distribution strategy is recognition of the fact that, given a particular list of tasks to be accomplished, these tasks must be performed, *regardless of the particular arrangement of intermediaries to be used in the channel.* Wishful thinking on the part of manufacturers often leads them to think that if only they could eliminate a certain distributor (by going direct or taking it over), their troubles would be over and their job much easier. Very often, however, exactly the opposite is true — and things become much more complicated instead. Quite simply, the tasks typically performed by that channel member must still be performed — but now the manufacturer has to do them.

Essentially, then, much of the focus of a distribution strategy revolves around deciding who will perform which tasks in the channel of distribution. A push strategy, for example, places the responsibility for promotion fairly squarely on the intermediaries' shoulders; a pull strategy means we shall ourselves carry the responsibility for this task. Similarly a "cash and carry" strategy means we require others to perform a financing function — we shall not do so ourselves. Quite clearly, distribution strategy is integrally related to our overall marketing strategy — perhaps more so than any other mix strategy element. In addition, it is important to recognize that distribution innovation often reduces to no more than a reallocation of tasks among channel members, suggesting that morphological analysis of task X channel member may be a productive way of generating distribution alternatives.

Definition and Implementation of Standards

Our final principle is, we believe, key to the successful prosecution of a strategy using intermediaries. To the extent that nonowned entities are used to perform some of the tasks incorporated in our strategy, we lose direct control. However, there is no reason why we should not define objective standards and measure and reward performance against those standards, just as we might attempt to do internally. Some standards may be based on more tangible outputs than others, but this practice — which is key to effective job design — is central to the successful management of a distribution strategy. The importance of this approach is usually better recognized by service companies than manufacturers. The success achieved over many years by companies like McDonald's or Holiday Inns occurred despite the fact that they faced opportunities not greatly different from those of less successful competitors. Anyone who has experienced filthy toilets at a gasoline filling station knows what happens when this principle is not in use.

Again, in simple terms, tasks should be clearly defined, standards made explicit, and intermediaries rewarded on the basis of how well they perform these tasks.

DEVELOPING DISTRIBUTION OBJECTIVES

For each element of the marketing mix we have discussed, it has quickly become evident that it is impossible to separate its development from that of the overall marketing strategy for the product/market we are considering. Nowhere is this more clear than for distribution, and it is nonsensical to conceive of such a thing as a distribution strategy except insofar as it comprises part of the overall marketing strategy. Some elements of that strategy are, however, uniquely concerned with distribution issues, while others are predominantly so, and it is upon these that we shall concentrate in this part of the chapter.

Functions of a Distribution Strategy

There are a number of functions which must be fulfilled by a distribution strategy. First, it should effectively coordinate the activities of various intermediaries so as to ensure the implementation of the overall product-market strategy. Second, it should define the standards of distribution performance we wish to attain. Thirdly, it should specify how our marketing effort will be allocated among channel members, and who will perform which tasks. These functions are summarized below, and they provide a useful set of criteria against which to evaluate a proposed distribution strategy or program.

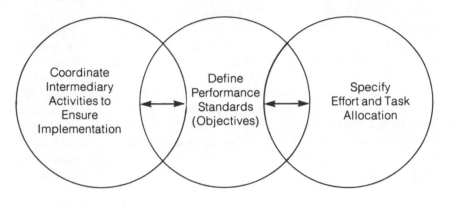

FIGURE 9-1   Functions of a Distribution Strategy

We now turn to the issue of defining distribution objectives, the step which must be performed before we can begin to set standards by which to monitor distribution performance.

Defining Distribution Objectives

There are two basic areas in which distribution objectives must be developed, and the standards which are set evolve directly from the overall strategy. The first category is fairly straightforward, and refers to the overall breadth of coverage to be attained. The second area is the establishment of service level objectives, given a particular network of intermediaries. This second area is, of course, enormously complicated and is also interrelated with decisions on breadth of coverage, as we shall see.

Breadth of Coverage

Breadth of coverage may be defined in several ways, *viz.*, percent of outlets selling similar products into the market by number, percent of outlets by turnover, percent of geographic area or units penetrated (by some agreed criterion) and so on, but each has different implications. Attaining very high percentages of outlets by number is usually a fairly arduous and expensive marketing job, but very high percents by turnover can often be attained with much lower percents of outlets, by application of the principle of selectivity and concentration (Chapter 3) to the characteristically skewed distribution of outlets arranged by sales volume (as defined in the classic 80/20 rule which suggests that 80% of volume is always generated by 20% of outlets and vice versa).

As Figure 9-2 indicates, the major considerations in deciding upon the target breadth of coverage are two, breadth of market target and frequency of purchase. Frequently purchased goods designed for a broad market target require very broad and extensive distribution. Frequently purchased goods are relatively inexpensive and are used in fairly high volume so that customers are unwilling to spend much time or effort searching for them. In consumer markets, the label "convenience goods" is used for this type of good, and such products as matches, cigarettes, toilet paper, chewing gum and candy bars all fall into this category. Widely used industrial supplies such as lubricants, paper clips and ball point pens would be analogous industrial products. High breadth of coverage is also sometimes called intensive distribution, the idea being that in a given area there is a high intensity of coverage.

In other situations, however, the target market is often much narrower than the cases we have just discussed — either because we are focussing on a very narrow segment of the market — perhaps a very high income group in one part of the country — or because infrequency of purchase means relatively few people are actively "in the market" (considering purchase) at a given time. In the extreme case, products or services marketed as highly exclusive may be designed to be distributed so as to make them fairly difficult to purchase — so-called "exclusive" distribution may mean only one outlet within a fairly large geographic area. More often, however, we find "selective" distribution where some but not all available outlets are used to give the desired coverage of a particular segment of the market.

The decision with respect to breadth of coverage, then, depends primarily upon the market being targeted, although other elements of the overall strategy are also important. Notice, however, that the customer target is already specified by the product/market strategy (Chapter 6) — so that a major element of the overall distribution strategy should already be given in general terms. This should be, then, an important starting point in distribution strategy development if we are to achieve implementation of the overall marketing plan.

Service Level Objectives

These constitute the second major area for objective setting — but it is a much more complex problem than breadth coverage. Earlier in the chapter, we listed just a few of the tasks which we might wish intermediaries to perform. Clearly, we shall not wish to set objectives in all these areas, since some may be unimportant to us. We must set some priorities, however, for too many objectives will almost certainly result in more confusion rather than better marketing.

In which areas should objectives be set? The answer to this question should flow in general terms from the overall product/market strategy. While we cannot cover all the tasks discussed earlier, we will take a few key examples to illustrate the principle of definition and implementation of standards, as well as indicating the considerations which leave us to set objectives in particular areas.

Average depth of line is often an important service level objective, particularly where there is heterogeneity of customer preferences. Consider breakfast cereals, for example. Let us suppose our brand comes in large and small sizes, and 80% of grocery outlets carry one size or the other, or both. We could in fact be in big trouble. Suppose 50% of our customers purchase the small and 50% the large size. If very few outlets stock both sizes, then (assuming some unwillingness to substitute sizes — and perhaps a willingness to switch brands) we could lose a very high number of potential sales. In these situations, a service level objective of ensuring minimum stock levels of *both* sizes may be vital.

Another example relevant to large durables or capital goods which require delivery and installation by intermediaries is the promptness and quality with which such services are provided. With many capital goods, and often for consumer durables, differences in price are much less important for many customers than rapid delivery and fault-free installation. If our core strategy (Chapter 6) is in any way related to these factors, then they become key service-level objectives.

One more example should suffice, and we could take that of personal selling activities by intermediary personnel. These are important in many industries, the automobile industry providing a good example. Here, the manufacturer's advertising and promotion has as one of its most important objectives generating dealer showroom traffic. Once potential customers cross that threshold, however, the dealer's salespeople take over the marketing job and are key to consummating the sale. Setting objectives with respect to dealer salespeople's selling skills is therefore very important to success in this industry.

ELEMENTS OF THE DISTRIBUTION STRATEGY

The service level objectives which are established for key tasks should exist regardless of whether we ourselves perform the task or intermediaries do. However, we must now decide which of the key tasks we have defined should be performed by ourselves, and which should be performed by intermediaries (Table 9-1). As we go through this process we are, of course, limiting our options, since some intermediaries may lack either the capability or the desire (and perhaps both) to perform some of these tasks.

TABLE 9-1   Elements of the Distribution Strategy

Distribution Strategy Element	Links to Relevant Business or Product/Market Strategy Element
Breadth of Coverage Objective	Customer Target, Core Strategy

Intensive
    Selective
    Exclusive	

Service Level Objectives	Core Strategy
Division of Tasks	Financial Strength, Mission
Choice of Intermediaries	Customer Target
Trade Marketing Strategy	Product/Market Strategy Field Sales Strategy Advertising and Promotion

These decisions on division of tasks touch the very cornerstones of the company's overall strategy. Notice that a decision tilted toward performing more and more of these tasks for ourselves is a decision to vertically integrate forward (Chapter 5); it is in effect a "make or buy" decision for some key tasks. This, in turn, may raise some very basic issues with respect to mission definition (Chapter 4) — e.g., we say we are a manufacturer *not* a distributor or financier. Further, changing mixes of tasks may produce very serious threats to existing distributors or distribution arrangements — e.g., when to sell direct *vs.* through distributors. Finally, there are some extremely important financial implications to the task division decision. As we undertake to do more ourselves, we typically (although not always) increase the fixity of our costs. We are trading off variable costs for more fixed costs, thus increasing our operating leverage, possibly penalizing cash flow as well.

In markets with large numbers of buyers and fairly small units of purchase, traditional wisdom and a variety of theoretical arguments suggest that the use of intermediaries is strongly favored. The growth of direct selling on television is leading to questioning of these views however, and new forms of interactive media offer the very real possibility of a revolution in the distribution business. Traditionally, however, there have been some clear advantages to doing things oneself *versus* using intermediaries. We have summarized the classical arguments for each approach in Table 9-2.

TABLE 9-2 Advantages of Direct *Vs.* Indirect Distribution

Direct (Performing Tasks Ourselves)	Indirect (Intermediaries Performing Tasks)
Control	Lower fixed costs
Greater ability to satisfy customers	Lower short-term negative cash flows
Additional value added	More flexibility, less rigidity
Lowers average capital intensity (for manufacturers)	Often lower cost

Choice of intermediaries is the final element which is central to the distribution strategy. It is important to note that, in many instances, no such choice may exist. In an economy such as the U.S. or the U.K., if the product is, for example, a convenience food with a broad consumer market, distribution via the large supermarket chains is essential to your success — the basic parameters of the overall marketing strategy leave virtually no degrees of freedom in the elements of distribution strategy discussed so far.

In other instances, however, we have considerable discretion over choice of intermediaries, and, once again, these are key choices. In effect, we are forming a coalition with other nonowned entities to jointly develop a market opportunity. For the most part, a marriage is likely to be preferable to a one-night flirtation, and many channel relationships tend to be enduring—and in some cases form the basis for subsequent merger and acquisition. When we have a choice, then, we should be looking for partners who share similar values, are open and flexible and capable of dealing with change and who can perform well the tasks that we cannot or choose not to perform. If the last condition is unmet, it may mean that remedying that situation becomes a key element of the trade marketing strategy, which we now discuss. It is also important to monitor the performance of our existing intermediaries to ascertain on an ongoing basis how well they are meeting the needs of our end customers. As these needs change over time, so must our distributors and our distribution strategy. If we fail to manage this evolution, we may render ourselves vulnerable to a competitor's distribution innovation. As we pointed out earlier in this chapter, such oversight is most likely to occur if we lose touch with our end customer and overrely on our distributors.

The trade marketing strategy is of course, an inseparable part of our overall marketing strategy, and it is at this point that the notion of any separate distribution strategy breaks down. However, the review, definition and division of key tasks incorporated in the earlier part of our discussion should greatly sharpen and refine this aspect of our marketing strategy. From this part of the exercise, then, may well develop some key requirements to be incorporated in our field sales strategy, our trade promotion strategy and so on. Returning to our automobile industry example for a moment, let us suppose that the oft-mooted change in motive power systems begins to look likely to take place — GM's experimental battery cars are unexpectedly successful, for example. We have already seen that dealer salespeople are key to car marketing. We may now decide that a key task is to give them and dealer mechanics a "crash" background on the new technology. "Selling" this to the dealers then becomes a key part of our field sales strategy.

SUMMARY AND CONCLUSIONS

In this chapter we have only been able to scratch the surface of an extremely important and complex aspect of marketing. We began by trying to identify some key principles of good distribution planning, hoping thereby to avoid some of the misconceptions which so often lead channel and distribution strategy astray. We spent the rest of the chapter outlining the key elements in designing and developing distribution objectives and strategies. In doing so we tried to emphasize several points.

First, distribution planning, like other mix planning, is very closely related to and constrained by the overall marketing strategy for the product/ market. Second, the challenge of distribution strategy often lies not so much in deciding what needs to be done — but in deciding who does what. Task definition in many cases flows from the marketing strategy, but the division of tasks is really the stuff of distribution strategy and planning. Third, we tried to emphasize the need for clear and identifiable standards as well as careful tracking of performance against those standards. Finally, we also made the point that many distribution-type decisions also carry very important implications for the overall corporate strategy in such areas as mission definition, posture toward vertical integration and financial strategy.

Finally, however, it seems wise to end the chapter on a cautious note. Perhaps because of their splintered nature, the distributive industries generally are a welter of change. Many innovations and innovators fail, but very often the impetus to change whole industries comes from an innovation in distribution. The insight that led to Baron Bich's success with the Bic™ pen or Hanes' success with L'Eggs™ pantyhose is very difficult to deal with except by extremely rapid imitation and out-investment. While careful analysis of distribution options and task redivision may reveal the possibility of drastic and rewarding change, vulnerability to shifting patterns of distribution remains a key problem for many firms.

REFERENCES AND FOOTNOTES

1. Philip Kotler, *Marketing Management: Analysis, Planning and Control*, Englewood Cliffs, N.J.: Prentice-Hall, 4th Ed., 1980, pp. 414-416.
2. Obviously, if we are a raw materials extractor, "intermediary" activity would include full manufacture. Our examples are less extreme, and are not intended to be complete.

10

PRICING
STRATEGY

Pricing is a vexing subject for most executives. For marketing managers, frustration arises because in some (operations-oriented) companies, these managers — and even market considerations — play virtually no part in pricing decisions. In many cases, however, the problems arise from the fact that a pricing strategy cannot exist alone, as an element separate from the product-market strategy, as discussed in Chapter 6. It is an integral and inseparable part of the overall marketing strategy, more intimately so than other element of the marketing mix. Those who speak loosely of pricing to gain share or to improve margin should be treated with great suspicion. Improving share or margin are appropriate strategic objectives for the product-market strategy *as a whole*. It is the function of the strategy *as a whole* to help achieve these objectives via implementing an agreed, integrated set of actions. Those who would ascribe to price *alone* the ability to achieve these objectives have a biased view of the importance of price *per se*, and a poor understanding of marketing strategy. At any rate, it is in this light that we shall examine pricing decisions in this chapter.

A further reason why firms so often seem to contort themselves over pricing decisions may lie in the light — and almost casual — treatment which has been given to the subject of pricing strategy by marketing scholars in recent years. While there have been some notable exceptions,[1] most basic marketing texts rely heavily on such classic works as Lanzillotti[2] and Dean[3] and have only experience curve notions to add.[4] Even though the underpinnings of our basic texts might be old, if they are theoretically sound we need not be concerned. In our opinion, however, many texts are highly deficient in that they focus too much on descriptive approaches, often at the expense of the normative. While there is clearly great utility in teaching how prices are set in practice, more emphasis on the right way to set prices is sorely needed.

In this chapter we shall address pricing strategy from the normative perspective. The approach developed, while theoretically correct, is also eminently practical. We systematically develop the steps in formulating a pricing strategy, indicating important relationships to existing pricing practices without enumerating them *per se*. Pricing strategy is then set in a strategic marketing planning context and thereby related to strategic direction of the product or business. Finally, we devote the last part of the chapter to brief discussion of pricing tactics, a key area for many firms.

STRATEGIC PRICING: A SYSTEMATIC APPROACH

Pricing has been and will always be the most highly leveraged decision variable with which marketing managers are involved.[5] In common with other marketing mix decisions, the marketing manager rarely has direct control over pricing, although he usually plays an important advisory role. The importance of pricing has, however, been underlined by bouts of heavy inflation during the 1970s, and it is therefore timely to re-examine pricing decisions and the basic assumptions underlying pricing strategy.

Conceptual Framework

To give our discussion of pricing a sense of perspective and direction, it is important to establish a sound conceptual basis. We shall therefore approach the pricing decision from the perspective of economics and exchange theory. Simply stated, this means that under conditions of full information, an exchange will only be consummated if both parties' lots are thereby improved, *viz*. utility of both parties is increased by the exchange. Less than full information enhances risks for participants, but expected values may easily be substituted at the cost of some errors.

This perspective serves to emphasize a number of points that are key to the discussion which follows.

1. Parties to economic transactions exchange value. Consistent with Lancastrian notions, we view any physical product as a bundle of utilities (values) affording potential satisfaction of a variety of needs.

2. Perhaps even more important, however, is recognition of the fact that value to the customer is potentially afforded by much more than the physical product alone. Time and place utility, for example are afforded by the distribution element of the mix, and there are countless other examples.

3. It should also be recognized that among the mix elements which generate value for participants to the exchange is information. Recognized as a necessary precondition for satisfactory working of markets,[6] it is clearly another important element of the mix.

The above framework therefore restates the oft-quoted but frequently (in practice) forgotten notion that to the customer, the product (and its associated marketing mix) is no more than its benefits.[7] Though a simple and basic precept, it is the heart of marketing's credo. Unfortunately, it has too often been viewed as an article of marketing faith rather than as a guide to marketing action.

Within the context of the framework discussed above, then, there are three key steps involved in the strategic approach to pricing that we shall advocate:

- Create value
- Measure value
- Capture value

Create Value

In our experience, it is very common to find a problem diagnosed as a pricing problem, when no such problem really exists. The easiest way for a salesperson to attempt to justify a lost sale is by bleating about the price, while suggesting that the price is too high is a very socially acceptable way for customers to reject an exchange. Upon reflection, however, it is evident that any rejection implies that, given no budget constraint, the buyer perceived the exchange unfavorably — the value offered for the price asked was insufficient or, alternatively, the price was too high for the value offered. Notice that one very important consequence of this perspective is that the seller need never have a pricing problem if he chooses to add value instead.

Of course, to add value demands a market orientation, often involves a modicum of added cost and runs the risk (in the limit) of excessive differentiation. Thus, too many firms choose the obvious and superficially easy solution of price competition. Addition of utility, benefits or value, however, remains as a much more desirable alternative for most competitors, if only because none but the low-cost producer can derive full benefit from price competition, and there is only one low-cost producer at any given time.

Value is primarily created and added by the use of the marketing mix, but it would be foolish to ignore the role of other customer-impinging functions in the process. The elements that would clearly be defined as nonprice elements in the marketing mix therefore would include product, promotion, distribution and service. Note, however, that other customer-impinging functions include manufacturing (*e.g.*, meeting delivery schedules, product quality), credit (*e.g.*, amount, terms, speed of approval), personnel/human resources (*e.g.*, selection, training) *et cetera*. Thus, as we saw in Chapter 6, it is vital to ensure that the marketing strategy coordinates and integrates not only the marketing mix, but also the contributions of other functions if we are to ensure that we deliver the designed benefits to our customer targets.

From a strategic perspective, strong arguments can be made that value augmentation is preferable to price competition. If groupings of benefits sought can be identified, the firm can segment the market, building a position in a niche from which its dislodgment will be more difficult, particularly on the basis of price. In contrast, advantage based on price and cost demands continuing vigilance in product and process technology, for one competitive breakthrough can destroy the foundations of the strategy.[8]

Measure Value

The foregoing section relates directly to the broad issues involved in formulating a marketing strategy and composing a marketing mix. It bears reiteration here, however, since it is upon the value created by the rest of the strategy that pricing must depend. In this section, however, we move directly to the crux of the issue: the measurement of utility or value created by the offer.

As a starting point, we shall argue that any attempt, no matter how informal, to measure utility is better than none at all. Thus, the "measurement" may be accomplished by nothing more sophisticated than the judgment of a far from dispassionate manager. Much better techniques are available, however, and these we discuss later in the Chapter.

Managerial Judgment

The most disciplined approach to the use of managerial judgment involves use of multiple raters, evaluating utilities of our own *and* competitors' total offerings on a set of scales which may be weighted if desired. In practice, even rankings seem to work quite well, although interval scale measures are clearly superior. Note that it is vital to the integrity of the process that we include relevant competitors in the evaluation. In some instances, we shall be dealing with factors for which there are no absolute or "objective" measures, so that an appropriate base for comparison is essential.

The bias inherent in use of managers' judgments is evident, and wherever possible, customers judgments should be substituted. Managers experienced in their markets, however, tend to have a fairly accurate grasp of what benefits are sought by customers. It is their judgments of relative importance and standing versus competitors' which should be viewed more circumspectly. A final caution in using customer judgments is to beware of polling our own existing customers. Failure to consider competitors' customers or even potential customers will mean that diagnostic information about potential new segments and markets for the firm will be lost.

Economic Analysis

Particularly where durable products and/or the supply of services are the focus of the strategy, straightforward economic analysis is a very powerful tool for the measurement of utility. In the case of the automobile, for example, life cycle costing has become the subject of a number of articles in the popular media, suggesting that in purchasing used cars, a slightly used "gas guzzler" may offer much better economic value than a high-priced but fuel-efficient import, even factoring in considerable fuel price increases. (Obviously, mileages travelled have an important influence on the outcome of such calculations). This very example, however, illustrates the flaw of a utility pronouncement based solely on economic analysis. In a perfectly rational world, prices of used gas guzzlers and fuel-efficient vehicles would reflect economic parity. The fact that they do not is strong evidence of the importance of subjective, psychological and sociological factors to many purchase decisions. Indeed, it has been suggested that in the U.S., ownership of a small car is now in many circles an example of inverse snobbery, which provides an excellent example of the importance of subjective factors, as does the "new values" executive conspicuously consuming mineral water instead of martinis.

More generally, however, wherever economic motives are important — in industrial marketing or many big-picket purchases, for example — or can be enhanced by the firm, economic analysis can play an important role in utility assessment. Comparison with next best alternatives gives a basis for potential price differentiation as well as insight into the likely difficulty associated with the marketing task. Nonetheless, it should be recognized that the utility to which we refer is perceived utility, as evaluated by the customer.

Customer Research

As noted under the use of managerial judgment, simple rating schemes administered to customers afford an improved means of measuring utility. More sophisticated means are available, however, and one of the most widely used is conjoint analysis or trade-off analysis.[9] Conjoint analysis requires ratings of alternative combinations of characteristics of the offering, and yields as output the utility (value) associated with each position on each characteristic. Since the approach is idiographic, it permits individual and segmental analysis of utility. These approaches are well described in the references cited, and are now in quite wide usage.

Capture Value

The next and final element in the systematic approach to pricing is to capture the value which has been created via the price offered for exchange. In general, the more of the created utility that the seller attempts to capture, the more limited his market will be. Take a hypothetical example of new form of motive power for automobiles. By setting a very high price-increasing system lifetime cost relative to that of the next best existing alternative the seller offers the buyer minimal incentive to switch to the new technology, thus limiting his market. Thus, at a high price for the system, only the most price-inelastic potential buyers (those with higher perceived utility) would switch. At lower prices, much greater incentive to switch would be created, with corresponding volume increases. The level at which the price is set relative to value created, then, is clearly an important issue — which we address in the next major section of the chapter.

Equally important to the level at which prices are set, however, are the means by which we attempt to capture the value which has been created, summarized in Table 10-1. Perhaps the commonest misconception about prices, after that of cost-based pricing, is that there is (or should be) just one price or a set price for the product. Such a single price is almost *prima facie* evidence of lack of competition in a market and is in fact rare in the "real world." The pricing tool which most closely approximates this notion, however, is *list price*. This may serve as a basis for actual prices, but in many industries list does no more than provide the base for discounting, and five percent of volume or less is done at "book." *Discounts*, then, are the basis for departure from list, and these may be based on volume, on function performed, on the requirements of a *bonafide* competitive situation or other such criteria.

TABLE 10-1   Pricing Tools: The Capture of Utility

List Price
Discounts
Allowances
Returns
Buybacks
Credits
Freight
Inventory
Bundling *vs.* Unbundling
Guarantees
Leasing
Price stability
Currency acceptable
Duties

Further direct and important influences on effective price levels include company policy on *allowances* (e.g., for advertising), *returns* and *buybacks*. In each area policies may vary from time to time, and such variations afford the advantage of lower visibility to the using firm than do changes in list price. Likewise, availability and terms of *credit* can be a less visible means of implementing pricing moves, particularly potent under inflation.

Policies with respect to *freight charges* and *inventory-carrying* are fairly obvious in their economic implications, while *leasing* offers possible variation over self-financing not only because of tax implications but also because of differing willingness to bear risk. *Unbundling* refers to marketing and pricing the different elements of one complex offering separately. The separate and extended *guarantee* offered by some automobile manufacturers provides one example of unbundling, an approach often advocated in the mature stage of a market life cycle, when customer wants are often more specific and demanding.

Finally, under inflation and fluctuating exchange rates, willingness to assume risk in terms of *price stability* and *acceptable currencies* can offer utility to the buyer and advantage to the seller. Negotiation on payment of *duties* is also an option, but its economic consequences tend to be unambiguous.

We have reviewed the above pricing tools for a number of reasons. One is the fact that the pricing issue is sometimes treated simplistically, and we wished to illustrate the potential complexity of pricing decisions. Thus, while we may have resolved the strategic issues in developing the pricing strategy, deciding how to implement the strategy is still very important, and a wide variety of alternatives is available. Second, it is worth reiterating the fact that there are both more and less obvious means of effecting price competition. For many competitors, less obvious approaches are preferred. There are some circumstances where we might wish to be most overt and explicit, thus clearly telegraphing our policy to the marketplace, but these would be less usual and generally tend to reflect positions of great actual (and, sometimes, would-be) strength. Finally, we should note that sometimes the issue of *how* utility is captured by pricing is more important than *how much* utility is captured — the issue we will address next.

PRICING AND THE PRODUCT/MARKET STRATEGY

The key strategic pricing decision revolves around *how much* of the value generated by the offering is passed along to customers and how much the firm attempts to retain for itself. How best to capture that value moves us into important considerations of pricing tactics, and involves deploying some combinations of tools such as those just discussed. In this section, however, we address the issue of strategy. Subsequently, we shall devote some attention to the issue of tactics.

As we saw in Chapter 4, inherent in most contemporary approaches to strategic marketing planning is some form of portfolio approach to managing businesses. Most of these systems involve classifying different kinds of business opportunity according to some measure (simple or compound) of market attractiveness and another of relative competitive strength. Based on the results of the classification, different strategic directions are suggested.

At the risk of some oversimplification, it would not be unfair to say that, from a marketing perspective, the major output of such classification systems takes the form of a market share objective, namely: raise share, hold share and divest share; for growth, maintain and shrink businesses respectively. Let us examine these strategic alternatives in terms of the utility/price framework.

Table 10-2 illustrates three possible interrelationships of value and price among two competitors in a segment. We will examine them sequentially.

Type 1

In this situation, competitors 1 and 2 offer comparable value/price ratios to customers, and we would expect stable share relationships among them; *ceteris paribus* $MS_1 = MS_2 = .50$. Note that such competitive equilibrium can occur even though 1 and 2 have very different prices, as long as value/price ratios are identical.

TABLE 10-2 Pricing Strategy and Market Share

Case	Utility/Price Relationship			Implication
Type 1	$\dfrac{\text{Competitor 1 Value}}{\text{Competitor 1 Price}}$	$=$	$\dfrac{\text{Competitor 2 Value}}{\text{Competitor 2 Price}}$	Share maintenance
Type 2	$\dfrac{\text{Competitor 1 Value}}{\text{Competitor 1 Price}}$	$<$	$\dfrac{\text{Competitor 2 Value}}{\text{Competitor 2 Price}}$	Share loss by 1 to 2
Type 3	$\dfrac{\text{Competitor 1 Value}}{\text{Competitor 1 Price}}$	$>$	$\dfrac{\text{Competitor 2 Value}}{\text{Competitor 2 Price}}$	Share gain by 1 from 2

Type 2

Here competitor 1 would be expected to lose share to competitor 2, the rate of loss bearing some positive relationship to the size of the discrepancy in value/price ratios. Note that the formulation serves to emphasize that there are many options available for "milking" or "harvesting" a business besides raising price, and all of these are related to reducing the utility of the offering by removing the support for one or more of its characteristics.

Type 3

This relationship is the one associated with a growth strategy With the value/price relationships indicated, competitor 1 would gain share from competitor 2. Notice also, however, that 1 could gain share while increasing price as long as value was increased more such that 1 improves its relative value price position. This is an important point, since simplistic interpretations of experience-curve economics or of implementing portfolio-based growth strategies often rely heavily on price competition, which is clearly only one strategic alternative for achieving share gain.

The key implication of the preceding, then, is that we must ensure value/price relationships among ourselves and our competitors are consistent with the strategic objectives we have established in this product/market area. If we have chosen increased share and volume as our primary objective, we must establish and maintain a higher value/price ratio than our competitors to achieve our goal. If, however, we shift objectives to emphasize cash flow, then a marked deterioration of value to price can be accepted, and will usually be planned for.

Since volume and share objectives are typically established in the light of the market and competitive circumstances that prevail at the time, we may conveniently summarize the general policy with respect to capture of value by the guidelines shown in Table 10-3.

STRATEGY AND TACTICS

The bulk of our discussion has focussed on pricing strategy, and this is appropriate for a book the concern of which is primarily with strategy. It is important to recognize, however, that most pricing decisions are tactical. This does not mean they are unimportant, because in sum these tactical decisions have enormous impact upon our market and financial performance. However, there are relatively few instances where manage-

TABLE 10-3   Guidelines to Value Capture

Decision	When
Pass along value to customers	- Well positioned in growth market - Demand is price elastic - Strong and aggressive competition - Threat of entry from potential competitors
Keep value to ourselves	- Market mature or declining - Demand is price inelastic - Weak or lax competition - Low threat of entry

ment has the opportunity to take truly strategic pricing decisions which can have major impact on competitive equilibrium. These instances are summarized in Table 10-4, opposite, and cover the vast majority of situations where the pricing decision can be considered strategic.

In situations such as those listed in Table 10-4, we may indeed be setting prices and to a very great extent determining where we are going to be positioned. Most of the time, however, the firm is more of a price-taker. Decisions that management must face are more deal-to-deal, and the prevailing level of prices is set by interaction among ourselves, our competitor and our customers. It is in these circumstances that the sound management of pricing tactics is essential, and can have major impact on the firm's performance. We now examine some key considerations in managing pricing tactics.

Improve Price Discretion

The first point is to recognize that we may have no price discretion whatsoever, and will be forced to accept offered prices, unless we can attain competitive superiority of some kind. Maximum price discretion is available to the competitor which has the highest perceived value and lowest cost. This is the ultimate position at which to aim, and is enjoyed by such com-

TABLE 10-4   Strategic Pricing Situations

Planning for or introducing new products

Planning for or entering new markets

Repositioning a brand or product in existing markets

When contemplating major change of strategic objectives

When facing major market change (new entrants, new game, etc.)

panies as IBM and Kodak in several of the markets in which they compete. With this degree of discretion, we may choose where we set our prices, depending upon the trade-off we choose to make between volumes and market share versus margins and profit. The moral here should be clear, for working to improve perceived value while reducing cost puts us in an enviable position with respect to pricing strategy and tactics. Many Japanese companies have learned this lesson well.

Pricing Information System

To manage pricing tactics well demands constant attention to price levels in the marketplace. A good pricing information system is a most useful aid to the necessary fine tuning that must occur. In many companies, the "lost business report" may provide the genesis for such a system. Customers are frequently obligingly informative to the losing salesperson, so that there is usually more information value in business which is lost than in business which is won.

Keep Pricing Flexibility

It is to the obvious advantage of the seller to maintain as much pricing flexibility as possible. Price discrimination is inherently more profitable and, since utility curves are idiosyncratic, is consistent with the strategic approach earlier advocated. The more customer demands vary, and the more that various nonprice weapons are available for use, the easier it is to implement flexible pricing tactics. If offers are identical, and buyers competing, it becomes much easier to run afoul of Robinson-Patman legislation in the U.S. and comparable laws in other countries. The ability to "design the order," however, while on the surface a costly approach, often pays profitability dividends because of the value-adding pricing flexibility which it endows upon the seller. Many contracting organizations have learned to appreciate and practice this philosophy.

Bundling vs. Unbundling

Generally speaking, it is more profitable to bundle than to unbundle. As a market matures, however, customers become increasingly demanding, as well as more expert in the technology of the seller's product. Unless sellers can innovate at a high rate, there is an inexorable shift of market power toward the buyer. Because of the need for organizational changes, as well as fear of poorer margins, market leaders are often reluctant to unbundle and often lose share to more focussed lower service level competitors. Such a pattern has consistently appeared in retailing ever since the evolution of the department store in the last century. If faced with weak competitors, we may be able to bundle longer, but in general we should be planning for unbundling and expecting ultimately to price the different elements of a complex offer separately.

Responding to Competitors

In general, we are well advised to avoid a directly comparable response to a competitor's offer. The less differential advantage we possess, the more likely we are to be forced into the inevitable position of having to respond in comparable terms. The final response of the delinquent marketer is, of course, commodity competition, where by definition such responses are the only ones available. To repeat a now perhaps redundant point, that type of competition is disastrous to all but the low-cost producer, who determines whether others live or die. By not responding in kind, we stand a better chance of avoiding the vicious circle of prices spiralling downward until they barely cover cost. However implemented, we should take pains to avoid confrontation. If a competitor moves on price, perhaps we can respond on credit or delivery (both less visible). If he acts on one size or grade, perhaps we can act in another. The point is to avoid increasing the buyer's bargaining power, for he is certain to use it. In responding to competitors' tactical pricing moves, it is a good idea not to make things too simple for customers or — if you like — keep things a little confused.

SUMMARY AND CONCLUSION

There is clearly nothing radically new in the preceding discussion. The origins of the framework lie in conventional microeconomic theory, and any merit lies in the organization of ideas discussed. Nonetheless, we are disturbed by the fact that all too often firms end up approaching pricing decisions from a completely nonmarketing perspective. Notice that costs have played virtually no part in our discussion. Quite simply, our value *vis-a-vis* competitors' sets limits on the price we can charge. Either we can produce and distribute the product or service for a cost less than this price, or we cannot. If we cannot, we should exit. It is in this sense that it is often said that price must determine cost, not *vice versa*.

In this chapter, we have attempted systematically to develop an approach to pricing which is not only soundly based in theory, but is both practical and consistently related to concepts of strategic marketing planning. Although some of the techniques of value (utility) measurement we have discussed may seem crude and imprecise, we remain convinced that in general approximate measures of the right variables are much to be preferred to apparently precise measures of the wrong—a situation which often prevails in pricing. Although the approach we developed may appear radical to some readers, it is based upon a most commonsensical observation—namely, that customers are willing to pay what they believe something is worth. They will not for long pay more than this, however, as long as they have alternatives to which they may turn.

Finally, we have tried to emphasize that while much brouhaha is made over pricing strategy, sound price management is frequently more concerned with tactics, yet has a most significant impact on performance.

REFERENCES AND FOOTNOTES

1. See, for example, Paul E. Green and Yoram Wind, "New Way to Measure Consumers' Judgements," *Harvard Business Review*, Vol. 53, July-August 1975, pp. 107-118, A. Gabor, *Pricing: Principles and Practice*, London: Heinemann, 1977, Robert J. Dolan and Abel P. Jeuland, "Experience Curves and Dynamic Demand Models: Implications for Optimal Pricing Strategies," *Journal or Marketing*, Vol. 45, Winter 1981, pp. 52-73.

2. A. D. H. Kaplan, J. B. Dirlam, and R. F. Lanzillotti, *Pricing in Big Business*, Washington, D. C.: Brookings Institution, 1958.

3. Joel Dean, "Pricing Policies for New Products," *Harvard Business Review*, Vol. 28, November-December 1950, pp. 28-36.

4. Derek F. Abell and John S. Hammond, *Strategic Market Planning*, Englewood Cliffs, N.J.: Prentice-Hall, 1979.

5. Peter T. Fitzroy, *Analytical Methods for Marketing Management*, London: McGraw-Hill, 1976, p. 228.

6. John A. Howard and James M. Hulbert, *Advertising and the Public Interest*, Chicago: Crain Communications, 1973.

7. Theodore Levitt, *The Marketing Mode*, New York: McGraw-Hill, 1969.

8. "Corporate Planning: Piercing Future Fog in the Executive Suite," *Business Week*, April 28, 1975, pp. 46-50.

9. Paul E. Green and V. Srinivasan, "Conjoint Analysis in Consumer Research: Issues and Outlook," *Journal of Consumer Research*, Vol. 5, September 1978, pp. 103-123.

11

MARKETING
IN ECLIPSE?

In the preceding chapters we have outlined a fairly developed but more or less conventional view of how marketing should be practiced. We do not pretend that many companies approach the ideals we have discussed. Many apparently do not wish to be truly marketing-oriented, and others, while desiring, will remain unrequited. In this chapter, however, we shall review some of the basic assumptions of marketing from a more iconoclastic perspective — for many of the basic ideas of marketing are now threatened or under fire.

THE IMPACT OF STRATEGIC PLANNING

Early in the book, I placed great stress on the longer-term responsibilities of marketing people, and noted the fact that all too often they are poorly executed, if at all. However, as we saw in Chapters 4 and 5, the decisions about which markets we shall do business in, and what we shall attempt to accomplish in those markets are key high-level strategy decisions, and in a well-managed company cannot be made without adequate information. Estimates of present and potential customer needs, and anticipated competitive activities, are vital to making the correct long-term investment decisions, yet in many firms marketing does a poor job, if it does one at all, in these areas.

There are many reasons for this phenomenon. First, it is an extremely difficult task in which even skilled and well-trained analysts and forecasters will often make mistakes. In organizations intolerant of failure it may be easier to ignore the job than to attempt it and fail. In addition, the time orientation of many marketing people is often inherently short-term. Fast customer decision cycles and accelerating product and technological life cycles reinforce the notion that marketing is a fast moving (and sometimes fast talking) action-oriented activity in which contemplation, analysis and planning count for little. Nothing could be further from the truth, yet the consequence of these attitudes is often to produce failure in the "thinking" part of the marketing job. Further, if attitudes are often unfavorable, this is fostered by lack of skill and training. Many marketing people reach their positions via the sales function, where traditionally there has been little emphasis on planning and much more on immediate sales results. Thus, the opportunity to acquire planning concepts and skills has often been limited. Finally, senior management's expectations of marketing have frequently compounded an already difficult problem. In many cases, chief executives look to their marketing people to produce only immediate results — in quarterly sales or market share reports, for example. With this perspective at the top, and the immediate pressures upon them, it is not surprising that many marketing people begin to focus their attention exclusively on the short term, for as we have seen, this was frequently their predisposition to begin with.

Unfortunately, however, in most companies the lead time required to develop major new products, to approve and erect new facilities or to develop major new markets is substantial. Thus, the chief executive is forced to make many decisions with long time horizons, decisions which can be made on the basis of hunch or intuition, but which are better predicated upon well-founded assumptions about the size and composition of future demand, as well as future activities of competiton. As corporate management becomes more oriented to thinking and planning strategically, they are increasingly moving toward the latter approach, and as they do so they are finding that many traditional marketing departments cannot or will not provide them with the information or insight they seek. As a result, they seek new individuals with different kinds of skills and backgrounds who can and will perform these functions. Drawn often from outside the firm, these individuals sometimes become very influential on the directon of the firm, and are variously known by such titles as corporate planner, strategic planner, business planner and permutations of such titles.

Our point is not to express hostility to these people or positions, for they are frequently called in to help perform what we defined as vital functions for the firm. It is merely to point out that had marketing people performed the long term part of their jobs better, the need for these new functions would have been much lessened if nonexistent. Simply, it matters not to the firm who does the job, but for the firm to prosper it must be done and done well. Yet, the hostility with which some marketers have received the influx of planners may be well placed, for they often end up doing many of the planning jobs which should have been done by marketing and were not. Some companies already have more planners than marketers, a trend which could continue if marketers cannot break away from their too frequent short-term preoccupations. In others, however, after a transition period, line managers are asserting their role in strategy development and the role of specialist planners is waning. One point remains clear: management neglects these strategic issues at their peril.

CUSTOMERS AND OTHERS

A further pressure for change which may have great impact on marketing as we know it today derives from the increasing recognition by top management that the firm serves in some way many different interest groups, certainly not customers alone. Among these groups, now fashionably called "stakeholders" by business policy theorists, are union officials and members, salaried employees, stockholders and lenders, the broader financial community, government and regulatory bodies, suppliers and so on. It is argued by policy theorists that the firm's decisions must take into account the varying and sometimes conflicting impacts on all these groups.

While there seems little doubt that marketing concepts and methods would prove useful and helpful in dealing with relationships among this broader set of interested parties, there seem to be relatively few proponents or practitioners of this approach. Rather, we see it illustrated for the most part in a somewhat piecemeal fashion which may, however, be adduced as support for our overall viewpoint. Among U.S. companies, for example, top management will hold briefings for Wall Street's investment analysts; other companies spend heavily on researching and advertising to the general public; some invest considerable effort in researching and attempting to meet the needs of their employees at many different levels in the organization. In sum, while it is uncommon formally to embrace a marketing approach to all the many parties who hold some kind of custodial interest in the firm, it is clear that many firms apply marketing principles to dealing with the problems. We expect such multilateral sophistication to become more common in the years ahead, as the pressures of an increasingly well-educated, affluent and informed citizenry manifest themselves through their various social outlets, whether in the form of unions, religious groups, consumer groups, individual investors or workers or via the formal political process. While customers will continue to be the key "interest group" other stakeholders will exert a powerful influence on the firm and its customers.

CUSTOMERS AND COMPETITORS

Another shift which poses increasing challenge for marketers seems already underway in the U.S. and, perhaps, elsewhere. That is the emerging recognition of the fact that competitors as well as customers must fit into the marketing equation. In the view of some, the concern of marketing with customers has become a possibly dangerous preoccupation, at least insofar as it has led to neglect of competitive considerations in making key strategy decisions. Certainly it is relatively easy to support the argument that few companies have been either committed to or skilled in competitive analysis and strategizing.

The consequences of such shortsightedness are likely to be marked, for there are a number of strong arguments to support the importance of competitive analysis and strategizing. The first and most difficult to refute is the market structure argument. Most large firms do not compete in perfectly competitive markets, and although the degree of imperfection varies, the majority of large U.S., European and Japanese companies compete in oligopolistic markets. With such market structures, firms' actions are inextricably interrelated, whether managers choose to acknowledge the fact or not. To the extent that markets are still growing or retain some elasticity with respect to strategic actions, the consequences of this interrelatedness may seem more escapable. However, oligopolistic competition in mature and relatively inelastic markets takes on most of the characteristics of a zero-sum game, and the implications for firm decision-making can escape none but the stupid or ignorant.

Recognizing these dynamics, however, typically does not motivate an immediate response, particularly in a large organization. Indeed, there is often a danger that the response may be so late that the organization's prospects have been severely curtailed. Nonetheless, with some reluctance and lassitude, more companies are beginning to pay much more attention to their competition.

A second reason to justify spending more time on analyzing and strategizing competitively flows from some very basic ideas embedded in marketing theory. As we have seen, the concept of marketing embraces the idea that the long-term prospects of the firm are best served if it consciously attempts to design offers and programs which meet the needs of customers, provided that the customer problems can be solved and benefits provided without disproportionate cost penalty. In competitive marketplaces, however, it would be impossible for firms practicing this policy perfectly to gain any advantage over rivals other than via price, provided homogeneous customer preferences were the case. In fact, however, heterogeneity, not homogeneity, of preference is the norm. In addition, product and offer design are also constrained by technology and economics such that superiority on all attributes of importance is exceedingly unlikely and, if attained, unlikely to be sustained.

As we have previously argued, then, a marketing strategist typically advocates that the firm should attempt to "differentiate" or achieve "uniqueness" so as to gain an advantage — "competitive," "unfair" or "differential" — over competitors. To do this, of course, demands considerable insight and understanding into what competitors have to offer. More important, however, developing the advantage typically involves costs, which would be unwisely incurred if any advantage were ephemeral rather than sustainable. Thus, to develop an advantage which can yield anything more than short-term benefits typically demands insight into the likely future offers of competition, which in turn suggests a vital strategic role for the gathering and analysis of competitive intelligence.

In addition to market structure, and competitive advantage, stage in market life cycle offers another good reason to increase the emphasis on competition. Note that in new or rapidly growing markets, the major tasks faced by the innovator and its early followers revolve around customers, intermediate and final. Initially, for the innovator, the focus must be upon growing primary demand, switching customers away from generic and often very familiar choices (e.g., natural fibers or ocean liners) to radically new (nylon or aircraft and airships). To be sure this is a big undertaking, but for many innovations offering major advantage to customers, competition from similar offers is at first unlikely to be a key issue. If the innovation is successful, however, its market grows, often at a fast rate, and, sooner or later, the early entrants attract a host of competitors. As the arena becomes more crowded, firms must focus not so much on primary demand but on selective demand, such that they must attempt to induce customers to buy *their* version of the product or service rather than competitors'. As we saw in the previous section, this means they must begin to focus their attention explicitly on competition to position and differentiate their offers. During this period the market is often "shaking out" weaker competitors, and a more stable segmentation structure and associated alignment of competition emerges.

As this process of market evolution takes place, an immense amount of learning occurs. Customers learn how the innovation can best meet their particular needs, and articulate those requirements more clearly and, sometimes, more forcefully — the very process which results in a defined segmentation structure. Analogously, firms surviving to later stages of the market life cycle also learn more of the demands of their customer base and adapt their offers to better meet its needs. As customer risk is reduced by information exchange, so competitive risk rises in relative importance, and as growth and elasticity disappear from the market, so does the firm's ability to deal with its competition (by whatever means) become the major challenge to its prosperity. Whereas in growth markets, dealing with customers is key, in many of today's slower growth markets competitive strategy is the crucial influence on the firm's prospects.

A final compelling reason to engage in some amount of competitive analysis is derived from the value of information in reducing risk. Clearly, competitors are a major source of uncertainty in most markets. Further, unlike a "passive" state of nature, they are active, intelligent and sentient players of the game with objectives often opposed to your own. It would be foolhardy in the extreme to make no attempt to learn of them and attempt to anticipate their actions. Perhaps it would be useful to draw an analogy from a regulated industry to illustrate the situation. In the pharmaceutical industry, new products have to obtain regulatory approval by the United States Food and Drug Administration prior to market introduction. The approval process is sometimes protracted, and it is certainly quite public. It would be ridiculous to operate in this market without attending to the pre-market introduction information which is available. Clearly, when easy to obtain, competitive information does affect management decision. Unfortunately, when obtaining analogous information may be more difficult, more costly, and subject to greater uncertainty, many firms "cop out" — they suffer the same kind of blind spot on this type of marketing expenditure that they do with many others — they see and manage only the *costs* and fail to consider and weigh against the immediate costs, the substantial but less tangible benefits which can result.

We already see greater attention being paid to the area of competitive strategy than in the past, and we expect these efforts to double and redouble in the years ahead.

COMPUTER-AIDED MARKETING

One of the most obvious changes we should discuss is the impact computers are going to have on marketing management. Clearly, the first two decades of computer wrought many changes in the management of both marketing and other functions. In marketing, the computer has permitted more sophisticated forecasting, much better approaches to segmentation analysis, improved allocation decisions and has led to closer coordination with manufacturing and operations functions (via better scheduling and execution) and finance and accounting (via better budgeting, costing etc.).

To date, however, computing power has resided mainly in large central processing units and with software and access remaining the domain of data processing departments. Further, the key line managers of this era developed their managerial skills in either the pre-computer or batch-processing periods. Both these conditions are now ceasing to prevail. First, the micro and minicomputer and reduced costs of hardware are driving a fairly rapid decentralization of computer power away from centralized systems and toward the user. Small systems are now within the scope of operating budget authority of many executives. Further, the proliferation of relatively low-cost general purpose software gives marketing executives the ability to improve greatly their planning and budgeting efforts without the delay and expense that was often associated with changing company systems. Finally, the new generation of managers is increasingly comfortable with on-line, real-time interaction with computers. For these reasons alone, we anticipate vast increases in computer utilization by marketing managers to be a key characteristic of the future of marketing. Marketing technology is, when all is said and done, an information technology, and the drive to computer-aided marketing will be both powerful and appropriate.

RESOURCE SCARCITY

The final point we should make — without raising Malthusian alarms — is the fact that it can be convincingly argued that the need for marketing arose from the evolution of relative affluence. While scarcity may be a very long way off, we should remember that the 1970s witnessed runups in a number of commodity price indices and shortage became a reality during several periods. Of course, Japan has never experienced the abundance of natural resources that long blessed the United States, and continues to endow Brazil and Australia, for example. As a consequence, Japanese companies have for some time realized their need to develop long-term supply positions and have adopted the necessary strategies. In the United States, however, concern over resources is more latter-day, and relatively few companies have yet emulated the approach of their Japanese competitors.

What we wish to discuss, however, is not the recent injection of resource planning into the long-term strategy of United States' companies, but rather the potential implications of scarcity for marketing as we know it today. As a colleague of mine half jokingly commented, marketing came about because customers were finally recognized to be a scarce resource. Could the end of marketing come about because the scarcity equation changes? If resources, rather than customers, become the crucial scarcity, then purchasing and resource planning activities may be elevated to far more lofty heights than we have seen to date, and the importance of marketing may lessen.

Those with post-Malthusian economics training, however, may take a less dismal view, for the economics of substitution and the influence of technological developments have repeatedly enabled us to evade such pessimistic projections, and seem likely to do so in the future. Nonetheless, it is worth remembering that the importance we attach to marketing in our current consumption-oriented competitive world economy may not prevail under some other scenarios.

SUMMARY AND CONCLUSIONS

Lest this final chapter prove too depressing thus far, we should note that despite the foregoing concerns, we anticipate a fairly healthy future for both marketing and marketing practitioners. As a new field, it is eclectic and ever-changing, and as long as it continues to embody the vibrancy and open-mindedness which has characterized it to date, there is little cause for concern. The consumerism of the sixties and early seventies posed, perhaps, the biggest threat to marketing. It not only weathered this challenge successfully, but there is, in retrospect, little doubt that marketing practice was much improved as a result.

The real challenges to the future of marketing will, we believe, be more likely to come from within the firm than without. They are, in fact, more likely to result from the faults of marketing managers themselves — or, in Pogo's immortal words, "We have met the enemy, and he is us."

These internal defects arise in most cases from factors we have already covered earlier in the book. A short-term focus, lack of understanding of the full role of marketing, lack of training (particularly in the financial area, the weakness that leads to the often-checkered relationship with finance and accounting) and failure to lead others to an appreciation of the vital importance of the marketing concept to the firm's future.

When all is said and done, however, these problems pale to insignificance when compared to the most serious flaw, the failing to believe in what is being practiced — i.e., the concept of marketing itself. Although sometimes motivated by sheer ignorance rather than cynicism, it is an unfortunate fact that many marketing people do not believe in marketing: they do not treat the customers as assets; they seem not to comprehend that without customers there is nothing. Those who give in to the pressures to neglect the customer fail to recognize that they are ultimately delinquent in their duty. Although there will always be pressures to do this, prospective marketing managers should recognize that to be truly professional requires of them not only intellectual mastery of the discipline, but the emotional commitment to hew to a path true to the marketing concept *despite* the pressures they will feel to stray. Otherwise, they are unworthy of their marketing title. Of course, we wish the firm to profit. The distinction of the marketing-oriented firm is that it recognizes the central role of customers in ensuring that end.

With those thoughts in mind, perhaps there is no better way to close this book than by offering for your consideration the words which hang on the wall inside a local business near my home in Connecticut. They read as follows:

The customer is the most important person in our business. The customer is not dependent on us, we are dependent on him. A customer is not an interruption of our work, he is the purpose of it. A customer does us a favor when he comes to see us, we aren't doing him a favor by waiting on him. A customer is a part of our business, not an outsider. He is not just money in the cash register, he is a human being with feelings like our own. He comes to us with his needs and wants, it's our job to fill them. A customer deserves the most courteous attention we can give him. He is the life blood of this and every business. He pays your salary. Without him we would have to close our doors. Don't ever forget it.

INDEX